The Divorce Party Handbook

THE DIVORCE PARTY HANDBOOK

How to throw an unforgettable Divorce Party when "Divorce Do Us Part"

CHRISTINE GALLAGHER

Copyright © 2015 Christine Gallagher, 2015.

All rights reserved.
Printed in the United States of America. No part of this book may be used or reproduced in any manner whatsoever without written permission except in the case of brief quotations embodied in critical articles or reviews.

ISBN: 9781522809241

Website: www.divorcepartyplanner.com
Email: ChristineGallagher@divorcepartyplanner.com

"A good divorce is better than a bad marriage."

Table of Contents

Introduction:	Why Have a Divorce Party?	ix
Chapter 1	Be Creative!	1
Chapter 2	Save the Date!	3
Chapter 3	Gifts Galore!	5
Chapter 4	Who to Invite?	14
Chapter 5	Yummy Food and Drinks	17
Chapter 6	Fun and Games	29
Chapter 7	Divorce Party Music	43
Chapter 8	Perfect Prizes and Decorations	46
Chapter 9	Buy, Borrow and Rent	53
Chapter 10	Last Minute Preparations	55
Chapter 11	Let's Party	59
Chapter 12	Funny Party Themes	60
Chapter 13	Sexy Party Themes	70
Chapter 14	"You've Got Friends" Party Themes	81
Chapter 15	Unique Party Themes	90
Chapter 16	Inspiring Party Themes	99
Chapter 17	After the Party	105
Chapter 18	Divorce Party Etiquette	107
Chapter 19	Looking Forward	112
Appendix		113

Introduction:
Why Have a Divorce Party?

Divorce is hell. Divorce can leave you feeling empty, depressed, not to mention irritated that your ex walked off with the J.A. Henckels 15-piece knife set. Divorce can also leave you feeling a profound lack of closure. The other "big events" in life—birth, marriage, graduation, death—have ritualized ceremonies to accompany them, and signify their beginning or end. These rituals are important. We need the support of our friends and family to get through life-changing events. We need a ritual, a moment in time that helps us understand the event in the bigger scheme of things—something to be enjoyed, or endured, but ultimately to be accepted and moved past.

In 2003 the writer of this book launched a trend – the Divorce Party – as a way to provide closure to the trauma of divorce. Now thrown openly by both celebrities and people across the world, Divorce Parties reflect a huge shift in our attitude to divorce. Divorce is no longer a mark of shame or failure. Today divorce is commonplace, openly acknowledged, and often applauded as an opportunity for growth, the springboard for a new and better life.

The Divorce Party can also counterbalance the way our culture handles divorce with a heavy emphasis on legality and conflict. Divorce, under most circumstances, is painful and draining. The party is a way to work through the emotional part of the transition. It's the final purging.

It should be noted that some people are uncomfortable with the idea of a Divorce Party. Let's be clear upfront. The event is not to celebrate the breakup of a marriage. The Divorce Party is a way to celebrate and launch the beginning of a new life.

In this book we will be looking at many types of Divorce Parties. Some people may be drawn to parties that involve lots of cathartic laughter and even outright silliness. Sometimes silliness is just what the doctor ordered. Others will want a more thoughtful event. This book is a guide to planning and throwing a successful Divorce Party with ideas ranging from one extreme to the other.

While many Divorce Parties are thrown by the divorcing person, others are organized by friends or family. It's recommended that even if you are throwing your own party, ask your friends and family to help, just as you would for a wedding. This is crucial—there is nothing better for a divorced person than to be reminded of the fact that their world has not actually ended, and that he or she is surrounded by people who love and care.

Occasionally a couple may host an event together. It can be a great way of letting everyone know that both partners are on the same page, are civil, and there is no need for people to choose one or the other, often a sad consequence of divorce.

Chapter One
Be Creative!

Begin by choosing a theme for your party. A theme sets the stage for all kinds of fun. The key is to be creative. Personalize your party. And don't hold back. Nothing is too crazy or too extravagant. Remember how much planning went into the wedding that marked the beginning of the marriage. Be prepared to put some of the same energy into the occasion marking the end. Have it be an event that everyone will remember.

The key is to build all the party elements around the central theme. For example, our party planning company DivorcePartyPlanner.com offers two turnkey parties with strong themes. One is a "Survivor Party". Built on the idea that the divorcing person survived a shipwrecked marriage, all elements of the party – food, décor, party favors - are built around a desert island theme. Another popular party we offer is a Lemon Party as in "when life gives you lemons, make lemonade."

Other successful Divorce Parties have themes built around something key to the breakup of the marriage. The goal is to defuse the pain by venting any lingering emotion, and even making light of something that has been very painful. Jamie's Divorce Party is a perfect example. Jamie had been married for 16 years to Tom, a popular successful car salesman who had recently taken up golf. One day Jamie found a photograph of a naked woman in Tom's briefcase. Tom hadn't been playing golf twice a week. He'd been with his new honey. Jamie changed the locks on the doors and filed for divorce. But she couldn't get over what had happened. Her husband had cheated and played her for a fool. And now she had to figure out what to do with the rest of her life. Her friends rallied around her and tried to get her out on the social scene again but Jamie was unhappy and wasn't prepared to be single again. She felt like she'd failed and the happy married part of her life was gone forever. Her friends decided something had to be done to shake Jamie out of her funk. They decided to throw her an unforgettable Divorce Party.

The friends chose the perfect theme for the party – a golf theme – in an effort to defuse what had happened and bring some much-needed levity back into Jamie's life. A mini driving range was set up for guests to hit golf balls that had Tom's face imprinted on them. Handsome instructors were hired to show the women how to handle the clubs. Custom cocktails named "Hole in One" were served, followed by shish kebabs, meat skewered on Tom's golf clubs cooked over a big outdoor firepit. A Divorce Cake had a triumphant bride on top holding a golf club in her hand, the groom tossed over the side of the cake, face down in the icing.

Jamie's party is a perfect example of why Divorce Parties are growing in popularity and becoming a modern day ritual. The party provided an opportunity for friends and family to gather around and show Jamie how much they loved and supported her in this painful time.

Whatever theme you choose, it's important to hit the right tone for the divorcing person. See chapters 12-15 for a wide range of party theme ideas.

Chapter Two
Save the Date!

There are no hard and fast rules on the best time for a Divorce Party. Some are held when the divorce decree is finalized. Others are thrown when the divorcing person is down in the dumps, often in the midst of a long protracted divorce. Whenever is chosen, it's usually best to schedule the party on a weekend night. Party guests will be free to let their hair down. Also steer clear of major holidays for obvious reasons. Your guests won't be as available.

Choose a Location

The location for your party will be pretty much determined by the size and budget of the event as well as the theme. Sometimes Divorce Parties are held in someone's house or apartment. Others take place in rented spaces like banquet rooms or clubs. There are pros and cons to each choice.

Private Home

Pros:
- Inexpensive.
- Relaxed.
- Can set own rules (to a degree).
- More spontaneity.

Cons:
- Have to rent all party equipment.
- Have to hire helpers (if it's a big event).
- Parking problems.

- Neighbors may complain.
- Bathroom facilities are limited (unless you rent portapotties).
- Dancing space is restricted.

Rented Party Space
Pros:
- Can simplify arrangements.
- Catering may be part of the deal.
- The serving of food and drink may be someone else's responsibility.
- Sound system is already in place.
- Dance area might be included.
- Parking is less of a headache.
- Better bathroom facilities.

Cons:
- Cost will be higher.
- Party will end at a pre-specified time.
- Activities might be more restrained.

Budget

Some divorce parties cost next to nothing, often no more than a night out on the town. Other people spend a lot of money creating an event that's as costly as their wedding. Considering the average U.S. wedding costs $26,000, that can be a lot of money. The bottom line is your Divorce Party can cost whatever amount you wish. If you want a big party, go for it. This may be the only Divorce Party you ever throw.

It's also important to be clear about who is paying for what. If you decide to throw your own party, friends might offer to contribute to the cost. But the responsibility ultimately falls to you. If your party is a dinner in a restaurant with friends, you can establish upfront if you want people to pick up their own tabs. The point is to make sure it's clear so there are no awkward misunderstandings.

Chapter Three
Gifts Galore!

Gifts are a must at a Divorce Party. These can be practical household items, making the party a Divorce Shower. Or they might be fun gifts or special treat gifts. For the big ticket items, considering pooling money together for a group gift.

Practical Gift Ideas

If the marriage ends in divorce, lots of household items often disappear along with the departed one. You go to iron a shirt for a business meeting and find the iron's gone. Suddenly you're filled with anger all over again at the ex who's still making your life miserable. You realize your ex took your beloved Italian espresso maker. Selfish to the end! You go out shopping and plunge into a funk as you feel like you're starting all over again.

In some cases the departing ones take some strange things. One husband took all the mirrors from the home he was leaving – he figured it would irk his ex no end. And he was right. Another thoughtful fellow stripped the house of light bulbs. One woman filched small items she knew would irritate her ex-spouse, like the nozzle on the end of the garden hose and the trash can under the kitchen sink, things she knew he'd have to spend time replacing.

The solution to avoiding this misery? A Divorce Shower can eliminate all of these extra negative emotions at a time when there are already way too many floating around. All invited guests bring a household item to restock the newly single person's home with the practical necessities of modern life. This makes the event a nice combination of a Divorce Party and a housewarming party. Some people even set up a Gift Registry to provide guidance for gift purchasers.

Usually a divorce registry is not the silver and crystal level of gifts, but downright essentials like sheets and towels, or mundane items like a kettle or even a selection of glues. It's also important is to replace those favorite little household items that we can't live without – like the ten dollar milk whisker to make homemade lattes. Or a waffle maker for cozy Sunday breakfasts. Replacing these comfort items can go a long way to restoring the newly single's person sense of equilibrium. In fact lavishing the party girl or guy with divorce gifts can be seen as one of the rewards of going through the hell of a divorce. He or she can wallow in retail bliss.

One sure bet for a woman is – he took the toolbox. You might consider having a few guests pool together and give her a nice toolbox full of the tools we can't live without. You can buy nice tool sets for a reasonable amount or you can go to a big hardware store like Home Depot and fill a colorful plastic bucket with an assortment like a hammer, drill, pliers, screwdrivers (flat head and Phillip's head), saw, wrench, assortment of nails, screws, nuts and bolts, tape measure. There is a company called DIYVA (www.DIY-VA.com) which specializes in tool kits for women. Not only do the kits have all the essential tools, the powder blue toolbox is nice to look at also.

Consider having one close friend go around the home with the party girl or guy and make a list of all the things that he or she needs to have replaced. Then establish a registry at a department store or home improvement center including everything on the list. Registering is even easier with the help of online registries. Remember to include the registry information on the party invitation.

Fun Gift Ideas

Another option is to have guests shower the newly single one with lots of fun gifts that will bring much-needed laughter to the occasion. Here are a few suggestions:

A Body-Shaped Bed Pillow

Sleeping alone can be a shock to the system for those who have been used to having a warm body in the bed every night. This Body-Shaped Bed Pillow is a nice transitional gift. You can cuddle up to it and find comfort in its presence. Available from many houseware stores including potterybarn.com.

A Divorce Blanket

A divorce blanket is similar in function to a baby blanket or a newlywed blanket. It is a symbol of comfort and self-nurturing and makes a nice commemorative gift. The divorce blanket can also be inscribed with a personal message. But bear in mind, if you inscribe the blanket with something funny or ironic, it probably won't last as long and will be tossed into the back of the linen closet, particularly if a new relationship comes along. So keep the sentiments to neutral acknowledgements of change like "One door closes, another one opens". Personalized blankets can be ordered at thingsremembered.com.

An Inflatable Man or Woman

This fun gift is not for everyone. Sometimes inflatable dolls are used as sex partners and that is definitely not the message you want to convey to the party girl or guy! Dress the doll in pajamas to avoid misunderstandings. What's nice about inflatable men and women is they let you rant and rave for hours and just keep smiling, without saying a word. You can buy them at chocolatefantasies.com.

The Perfect Man or Woman

These 12" high dolls are lots of fun. They are programmed with all the flattering statements that we yearn to hear from our real life partners, but never do. For example, the Perfect Man says things like, "This evening, let's just lie in bed and talk all night" while the Perfect Woman coos, "You're perfect just the way you are, I wouldn't change one thing". Available at amazon.com.

Pink Light Bulbs
Buy him or her a basketful of pink light bulbs. Replacing any harsh lights in the home with soft flattering light can be great cheap therapy. The last thing a newly single person needs is to glance in the mirror and see a sagging bag of wrinkles. Make the environment soft and flattering, a cocoon of soft light. While it may be true that life can't be looked at through rose tinted glasses, you can create a mood that is the next best thing.

Tango Lessons
Many people have a secret urge to learn to tango. Why not seek out a dance school that offers tango for beginners and buy your divorcing pal a package of tango lessons? It's good exercise. And a side benefit may be that it offers an easy way for them to be around new people without actually having to speak.

A Teddy Bear
There are so many lovable bears out there, one to melt everyone's heart. While it might sound childish, some adults do find solace in digging out their favorite stuffed toys at a time of great stress. What better time to acquire a new companion? For a good selection, check out justteddybears.com.

A Voodoo Doll
A voodoo doll can be used by the divorcing person for venting any residual angry or negative emotion, though it's preferable and certainly healthier to do this with a good helping of humor. Amazon.com offers a wide variety of dolls for sale.

Warm Bed Socks
It sounds simple but wearing warm woolly socks to bed can be an easy and effective way to comfort the soul.

A Puppy
A sweet pet can provide an instant object to love and can get your friend outside and exercising. Most cities now have dog parks which

often double as safe public places for singles to mingle. Check first that the party girl or guy is ready for a dog before making the purchase.

A Membership to an Online Dating Site

Choose a dating site one that is well known and reputable. While he or she may not find Prince or Princess Charming, they might have plenty of fun kissing (or not) lots of toads and toadesses. There's nothing like the ease of online flirting to whisk away any vestiges of sadness. At the very least, it's heartening (and kind of terrifying) to know there are SO many people out there looking for love.

A Commemorative Plate

For those with a mischievous sense of humor, a commemorative divorce plate might be just the ticket, especially if you gave the recipient a wedding plate. One idea is to have the plate feature a photograph of the divorced couple with a big ugly rip down the middle and the words "Celebrating the breakup of Sandra and Tony".

A Fun Read

There are tons of books on the market for the divorcing person who might welcome an amusing take on love, loss and pain. Here are a few favorites:

- *The Life and Loves of a She-Devil* – Fay Weldon
- *The First Wives Club* – Olivia Goldsmith
- *Waiting to Exhale* – Terry McMillan
- *Heartburn* – Nora Ephron
- *Frankenstein* – Mary Shelley
- *The Woman's Book of Divorce* – Christine Gallagher

Penis Punchbag

This is an x-rated variation on a penis *piñata*. It is a 5 foot tall inflatable which stands like a punching bag ready to receive guest's punches.

A Just Divorced T-Shirt
This might be something fun to wear next time he or she heads to the mall. A definite conversation starter.

A Single Guy/Single Girl Gift Basket
These fun baskets contain all kinds of essentials for the newly single. Simply fill a basket with movies, snacks, lingerie, chocolates and lotion.

Group Gift Ideas
Bedroom Makeover
The bedroom is the epicenter of the marriage where a lot happens, or doesn't in too many cases. Sleeping in a bedroom after a partner has gone can be a sad and lonely experience. Recreating the environment can be excellent therapy. Actress Kim Cattrall of TV's "Sex and the City" reportedly redid her bedroom in all pink after her divorce. It's a simple but effective way of reclaiming a space as one's own.

A bedroom makeover is best done as a group gift. The friends might paint the bedroom together. They might help the divorced one buy a new mattress and all new linens. When choosing the bed linens, don't skimp. Go for high quality sheets such as Egyptian cotton in a classy timeless design. The divorcing one will soon love going to bed at night in a room clear of memory and association.

Plan the party for a weekend and do all the hard work during the day. Then as the sun starts to dip, crack out the party food. Make it simple. Takeout is much advised after a day of hard work.

Fabulous New Underwear
Great underwear can never be underestimated. Just wearing it can give a feeling of confidence and attractiveness. Most department stores sell luxurious lingerie. Or go to a specialty store like Victoria's Secret.

A Makeover
You have to be careful with a makeover gift because you don't want to give the message that he or she needs a makeover. Make the point that a makeover can be very ego-boosting, not to mention a nice statement that one is out there and moving on. Check with salons or spas in your area and select one of the many packages that are offered – anywhere from a 2 hour hair and makeup session to an all-day pampering with head to toe exfoliation, the full renewal package.

Plastic Surgery or Dental Cosmetics
A new profile or a bright new smile can be a huge ego booster. This gift should only be considered if it's something the divorcing pal has been wanting to do for a long time. It can be costly, so have a bunch of guests chip in.

Delivered Meals
A month of delivered meals is a great treat and particularly meaningful for newly single people, especially if they're used to cooking for two. It helps to bypass the melancholy of cooking for one or eating alone in a restaurant. Having good well-balanced meals delivered is also healthy and a great energy booster.

Most large cities have a huge range of meal delivery options. We're not just talking about calling up a local restaurant and ordering off the menu. You can have organic meals delivered, vegetarian, vegan, or even old-fashioned comfort meals. Meat loaf and mashed potatoes can be very satisfying, especially if eaten while watching a good movie.

A Singlemoon
The honeymoon is a long forgotten memory. Now is the time for a singlemoon. Consider pooling your money together and helping your divorcing friend realize their dream trip of a lifetime, whether it's sailing up the Amazon, a trip to Nepal or to Peru's Machu Picchu.

Active divorcees might love a biking holiday in France, a trek up Mt. Kilimanjaro, dog-sledding in Maine, rock-climbing along the Potomac River or sea-kayaking on the Pacific coast. Online sites like TrustedAdventures.com offer great adventure trips for people needing to get away from their everyday lives.

One excellent idea is a week on a cruise ship or at a singles resort like Sandals or Club Med. With lots of parties and tons of great food to eat, this break from real life may be just what the doctor ordered.

For women, how about a cruise to Alaska? The men still far outnumber the women there and hopping into any Alaskan bar can be a great ego boost, particularly for New York women who are used to jostling through hordes of single women whenever an unattached heterosexual male is around.

Before you spring for a trip however, think it through. Some people in the aftermath of a breakup won't like to travel alone and the last thing you want to do is to launch them to some faraway place where they end up feeling sad and lonely. This can trigger a backslide to reminiscing the days of couplehood. Consider booking the trip for two so they can invite someone to go along with them.

For single travel packages, check out:

- MeetmarketAdventures.com
- Solotravelportal.com
- Singlestravelinfo.com

For women travelers only, check out:

- WildWomenExpeditions.com
- Women-Traveling.com

A Quickie Divorce

For that special case where the divorce is taking way too long, consider giving the wannabe-divorced a trip to the Dominican Republic for a quickie divorce. While Las Vegas used to be a big divorce destination, now you have to be a resident for at least six weeks prior to filing, and then stay for six weeks after the filing until the divorce becomes final. The Dominican Republic offers the service without a lot of hassle or wasted time. See dominicandivorce.com for more information.

Chapter Four
Who to Invite?

Try to invite at least 20 people. A good-sized group is more likely to get the party jumping. Also be sure you choose people who have a good sense of humor. If they think the idea of a Divorce Party is bizarre or in bad taste, zap them from the guest list. You need people there who are totally behind the concept of the party.

Many Divorce Parties restrict the guest list to females only. It's a primitive regrouping, women supporting women. Be careful if you are inviting both sexes. The last thing a recently separated person needs is to be around a bunch of happy couples.

One interesting idea could be that every guest has to invite a companion of the opposite sex. These could be dangled as potential future dates for the party guy or girl. The "dates" might come later in the evening, after the party games are over and everyone is happy. Be sure you choose guys or girls who can get into the right spirit.

Also, be sure all the guests are prepared for the tone of the event. If any of your guests have just met the guy of their dreams, tell them to zip it. This isn't the time to tell everyone about their new gorgeous hunk of maleness. If any guests are soon to be married, tell them to cool it with glowing reports of their impending nuptials. And be sure to put a gag on any sad sacks who are going to draw the party girl or guy into a corner to ask, "Tell me what went wrong?"

You probably don't want to invite relatives of the departed partner, unless they are firmly in the divorced one's corner. And don't invite the departed one, unless it's a joint party. If there are children involved, keep them away from this occasion. Little kids just won't get it and it could be very confusing for them.

And don't forget, if guests offer to help with the event, let them. The more the work is spread around, the better it will be for every one.

Party Invitations

Remember this is a major event in a person's life, so don't skimp on the invitations. Make them fun yet formal. And include the following information:

- Date and time.
- Location. Attach a map if necessary.
- Suggested Attire. This is important. There's nothing worse than showing up in jeans and everyone else is dressed to the nines.
- Gift Information (if appropriate).
- RSVP Instructions.

You can make your own invitations especially if you're handy on the computer. With the software packages available today you can produce an invitation that's nearly professional quality. You can also order invitations over the Internet or take your design to a printer and have them made for you.

Make sure your invitations establish the spirit of the party. Here are a couple of samples:

> Mary Smith
> is pleased to announce
> the end of her marriage to...
> what was his name?
> Please join her in celebrating her liberation
> 7p.m. Saturday July 16th.
> 3, Stanley Place
> RSVP: 888-555-1267

*

You are invited to Sheila's Divorce Shower!
8pm Friday May 3rd.
25 Mulberry Crescent
LET'S PARTY!
RSVP: 888-555-2398
Party attire
Sheila Barnes is registered at Target.com

Ask Some Distinguished Guests

Did you know that if you send a wedding invitation to the President and First Lady, you'll get a note back on White House stationery expressing their regrets that they can't make it? Now if enough people send in their divorce celebration invites, don't you think they'll come up with some kind of stock acknowledgement? To be part of this growing movement, send your invite to: The Honorable (first, middle and last name of sitting president), 1600 Pennsylvania Avenue NW, Washington, D.C., 20500.

Include Magnets

Some wedding invitations come with personalized magnets which make cool save-the-date mementos. These can easily be ordered to tuck in with your Divorce Party Invitation.

Check out Topweddingsites.com for more information on ordering the magnets which come in a variety of colors and styles and allow up to three lines of text.

Chapter Five
Yummy Food and Drinks

The theme of the party will determine food and drinks. Whenever possible, go all out on your party food. You don't have to count calories at a time like this.

Your food can be catered, can be potluck, or it can be provided by the party host. First, decide what type of food you will be serving. Use your creativity to tie your menu in with your theme.

Next, decide if it will be a buffet or will guests sit at tables? If you have a sit down meal, you need to decide if your guests will serve themselves from food tables or will you hire waiters? If you have servers, plan on one for every six guests.

Buffet tables are the best choice for a party. They can be made to look good, they're functional and they allow people to continue to circulate. Plan your buffet carefully. Make sure it is substantial and filling because you don't want hungry guests leaving early so they can go for dinner. And for those who don't eat meat, provide some interesting alternatives other than boring carrot sticks.

Your menu choices can be outrageous or subtle. Have lots of fun with your food and be creative tying it in with your party theme.

A "Split" Theme

A favorite idea for Divorce Party food is a Split theme. This menu can include anything that is "split", items like Split Chicken Breasts, Split Pea Soup, Banana Splits and Banana Split Cake.

Split Pea Soup (Serves 10)
8 cups water

1 pound dried split peas (about 2-1/4 cups)
1 to 2 lb smoked ham
1 med onion
1 tsp salt
1/4 tsp pepper
2 or 3 carrots chopped
2 or 3 stalks celery chopped
Heat water and peas to boiling. Boil for 2 minutes, then remove from heat and cover. Let sit for 1 hour. Add ham (whole piece), onion, salt and pepper. Cover and simmer until peas are tender, about 1 hour.
Remove ham and trim meat from bone. Cut ham to 1/2 inch pieces. Stir ham, carrots, and celery into soup. Cover and simmer until veggies are tender, about 45 minutes.

Caramelized Banana Split (Serves 4. Multiply as needed.)
2 ripe bananas
1/4 cup coarse or granulated sugar
2 flavors ice cream
1/2 cup chocolate sauce
1/2 cup marshmallow sauce
1/4 cup pineapple sauce
1/4 cup chopped peanuts
4 mint sprigs, for garnish, optional
Cut bananas in half lengthwise and then in half again crosswise. Pour sugar onto a small plate. Dip the cut sides of the bananas in the sugar, and caramelize under the broiler or with a blowtorch.

Place a scoop of each flavor of ice cream in a martini glass. Place 2 pieces of caramelized bananas at the back of the glass like rabbit ears. Drizzle with chocolate sauce, then spoonfuls of marshmallow sauce and pineapple sauce, then sprinkle with chopped nuts. Garnish with a big sprig of mint.

What to serve as a drink? Consider offering your guests a signature cocktail, Splitsville, with this menu.

Sole Theme
Another neat idea is to play with a "sole" theme for food, as in you're now going solo. Choices could be dover sole...or soul food, labeling it of course as "sole food". Typical soul/sole food is fried chicken, macaroni and cheese, collard greens, okra and cornbread.

Comfort Theme
What a perfect opportunity to indulge in unbridled comfort food. Popular comfort foods are mashed potatoes made with lots of cream and butter, meatloaf, macaroni and cheese with chunks of lobster, or toasted cheese sandwiches with homemade tomato soup. Don't forget to have really good crusty hot bread with ice cold pats of butter. Dessert is easy. A crowd pleaser is Ben and Jerry's Heath Bar Crunch or, if you have a backyard firepit, have guests make s'mores.

Sexy Theme
Since sex has probably become a long forgotten pastime, one way to get you in the mood is to serve hedonistic food heavy on pleasure. Menu items might include oysters Rockefeller or pasta with robiola and truffles. Foods with overtly sexy qualities include strawberries, especially when hand fed, avocadoes (a natural remedy for erectile dysfunction), artichokes (think sucking and tearing with teeth), asparagus presented fresh and erect in a nice bowl, and figs split open in a very friendly manner.

Dessert should be heavy on chocolate such as chocolate mousse or chocolate tart. Wash down with a sexy rum-based cocktail.

Pun Extravaganza
The Pun Extravaganza party menu is a glorious mélange of pun heavy foods. The obvious centerpiece is a big roast turkey. Supplement with Freedom Fries, as well as anything with lemons

and nuts such as green beans tossed with both. A great drink choice is Ale-imony. And for an extra bang, throw in anything the departed one didn't like to eat.

The Cake
You MUST have a really great cake. After all, you probably had a great wedding cake to launch the marriage. You need an equally memorable cake to mark its end. Figure out how many people you will be serving before you order the cake. They are usually priced per slice. You might splurge and have your baker make a wedding cake with a special decoration on the top.

A divorce cake might have a female figure standing victoriously on top of a male figure or a bride standing next to a groom face down in the icing. Another idea is to have a bride and decapitated groom on top. The head is hidden in the cake somewhere and whoever finds it wins a prize.

Other cakes might have something written on top such as "and she lived happily ever after…without him."

Celebrity cake maker Sylvia Weinstock created a divorce cake for a client she'd previously provided with a wedding cake. The divorce cake was sliced down the middle in two perfect halves, his and hers.

For pictures of some really great Divorce Cakes, check out oddstuffmagazine.com, October 10, 2010.

Drinks

You can even make this occasion extra special by offering your guests some wild cocktails. They're guaranteed to get your guests in the mood to party. If you serve wine and beer, don't skimp by buying cheap brands. You can buy quality labels at a reasonable cost at superstores like Costco.

Try to hire someone to be the bartender. Or have one of your friends be the designated drink mixer. Offer just two or three cocktail choices so your bartender doesn't lose his or her mind. Write the names of the drinks you're offering on a card and place it over the bar area. And include the main ingredients so they know what the heck they're imbibing. And be sure to have someone in charge of clearing glasses that are left lying around.

Serve a Signature Cocktail

Signature cocktails are popular with the wedding crowd. Why not do the same with your event and offer your own signature Divorce Party Cocktail? Make sure it has a cheeky name, and consider making a festive sign announcing it at the bar. Choose a name that will tie in with your theme. Here are a few suggestions:

Charlotte's Raspberry
(the name of party girl or guy giving a raspberry to the departed one)
2 oz. sloe gin
2 dashes raspberry syrup
2 dashes lemon juice
1 egg white
Put all ingredients in a shaker with ice. Shake well, strain into a chilled cocktail glass. Drop a raspberry in the glass for a special touch.

The D.C. (Divorcee's Cocktail)
3/4 oz Dubonnet
3/4 oz gin
1 Dash of cherry brandy
1 Dash of orange juice
Shake all ingredients with ice, strain into a cocktail glass, and serve.

The Last Kiss
2 oz chocolate liqueur such as Godiva or Crème de Cacao
1.5 oz vodka

Hershey's Kiss
Pour all ingredients into a shaker with ice, shake well, and pour into a chilled cocktail glass over a single Hershey's Kiss.

So Long Sucker
1 1/2 oz rum
2 oz cranberry juice
2 oz orange juice
Pour all ingredients into a cocktail glass over ice. Stir and serve with an orange slice.

Hanky Panky Cocktail
1 3/4 oz gin
3/4 oz sweet vermouth
1/4 oz Fernet Branca
Stir in mixing glass with ice and strain. Add orange peel. Serve in a cocktail glass

The Lifeboat
Decadent Recipe:
1 oz vodka
1 oz Kahlua or other coffee liqueur
3 oz coconut milk
Serve chilled over ice in a tall glass.

Low Carb Recipe:
1 oz vodka
1 oz coconut milk
1 oz strong coffee
1 pkg sugar substitute
1/4 tsp vanilla
Served with ice in a tall glass.

The Gay Divorcee
1/2 oz dark rum

1 oz light rum
1 oz fresh lime juice
1 oz honey
Shake in a cocktail shaker then strain into a cocktail glass.

So Long Sucker
1 1/2 oz gin
1 oz fresh lemon juice
1 tsp sugar
Ginger ale
Shake in iced cocktail shaker, strain into a highball glass. Top with ginger ale.

Splitsville
1/2 oz banana liqueur
1 oz light rum
3/4 oz orange juice
Shake in a cocktail shaker, then strain over crushed ice in a cocktail glass.

Alimonytini
2 ½ oz gin
½ oz dry vermouth
Orange or Angostura bitters
Pour over ice cubes and stir. Strain into a chilled martini glass. Garnish with an olive or lemon twist.

Sexagaintini
1 oz vodka
1 oz schnapps
1 splash 7-Up or soda water
Stir ingredients. Strain into a chilled martini glass.

The Take It All
This drink is appropriately green.

3oz Green Crème de Menthe
3oz Amaretto
2oz lemon juice
Stir then serve over ice in a highball glass.

Adios MotherFuc*er aka The AMF
½ oz vodka
½ oz gin
½ oz rum
½ oz tequila
blue curacao
sour mix
7-Up
Stir ingredients, then serve over ice. Garnish with maraschino cherries or lemon wedges.

Hit the Road (Jack)
1 ½ oz light rum
¾ oz lime juice
¼ oz sugar syrup
Shake with ice cubes in a cocktail shaker. Strain into chilled glass.

Liar Liar Pants on Fire
This is a nice fire red drink.
1 oz gin
½ oz Benedictine
½ oz cherry brandy
½ oz Cointreau
dash Angostura Bitters
5 oz pineapple juice
½ oz Grenadine
Shake with ice in a cocktail shaker. Strain over ice in a tall glass. (Serves 3)

Serve Punch

If cocktails are not your thing, serve punch. If you don't have a large punch bowl, you can buy a cheap one in most department stores or you can rent a fancy one from a party supply company. Almost any punch will work, but here are three punch recipes, a luxurious punch, a budget-minded punch, and a fun Divorce Party recipe. Make sure you have extra chilled ingredients standing by in case your guests are thirsty and you have to replenish the bowl!

Elegant Punch (Makes 16 cups)
1/2 cup Chambord raspberry
1 cup Triple Sec
1 cup brandy
2 cups pineapple juice
1 liter of ginger ale
2 bottles dry champagne

The night before the party, chill the ginger ale and the dry champagne. Combine the Chambord, Triple Sec, brandy and pineapple juice in a bowl, cover, and chill overnight. When ready to serve, combine all ingredients in a crystal or glass bowl. Add lots of ice cubes, and serve with a ladle.

Traditional Punch (Makes 20 cups)
2 cups vodka
4 cups unsweetened pineapple juice
4 cups unsweetened cranberry juice
64 oz ginger ale
2 cups sugar

Mix all ingredients together and serve in a large punch bowl with plenty of ice. Adjust vodka and sugar to your taste.

Rum Baby Rum
1 quart orange juice
1 quart pineapple juice

1 quart club soda
6 ounces of freshly squeezed lime juice
1 liter of white rum
Mix ingredients. Refrigerate until ready. Serve over ice. Garnish with maraschino cherries or lemon and lime wedges.

Martini Bar
Another way to go is to have a Martini bar where guests can order from a range of zingy martinis. In larger cities, there are companies who will come and set up a Martini bar for you and provide servers. If you do it yourself, check out websites like martiniart.com for martini recipes.

Non-Alcoholic Drinks
Provide soft drinks for the designated drivers in your crowd as well as those who don't drink alcohol. These should include fruit juices (orange, apple, cranberry) and a range of sodas including decaffeinated and diet.

Stocking the Bar
As well as a good supply of your selected drinks, here is what you will need:

- Glasses to match the drinks being offered. (At least 3 per person.)
- Blenders (2). If serving mixed drinks, this will keep things moving.
- Cocktail shakers (2)
- Cocktail strainers (2)
- Bottle openers (2)
- Wine bottle openers (2)
- Cocktail napkins
- Ice
- Garnishes like olives, lemon and lime wedges

Tips on Drink Consumption

If you're using a caterer, they can advise you on the quantities of drinks you should buy. They may even supply the liquor for you. Here are a few guidelines to bear in mind regarding average guest consumption:

- A liter of alcohol makes 20-22 drinks.
- A bottle of wine provides five servings.
- A case of champagne will fill 75 glasses.
- For a four hour event, estimate 4 drinks per person.
- For wine with dinner, estimate two or two and a half glasses per person.

A Toast

Make time during your party for a Toast. Make up your own or choose one of the following:

Better a tooth out than always aching.
Marriage is the only war in which you sleep with the enemy.
Husbands are like cars. They're all good the first year.
If they can send a man to the moon, why can't they send them all?
Time does heal all wounds, but who has time to wait?

Caterers

So you've decided to have a caterer handle the menu. Ask around for recommendations. And always personally interview a caterer before you make a commitment. Be sure to ask for references.

Most quality caterers will make up a special menu for an event with a theme. Give them free rein. You never know what they may come up with. Good ones are extremely creative though feel free to offer your ideas.

Questions to ask a Caterer:

- What are specific hourly charges for all staff? How many hours would they work? What about gratuities? Overtime charges?

- What choices do you have for glass, silver, china, linens?
- How do they handle the liquor?
- Is a cake included? If not, what is the charge? Can you provide one yourself?
- What is an estimate on total costs for your party including all the food?

Chapter Six
Fun and Games

It's important to keep your guests entertained at your Divorce Party even if it's just some fun games. If the budget permits, spring for an entertainment. Go online to find information on companies that offer party entertainers in your area. And make sure this offers the right tone for your particular crowd.

Stripper
Strippers aren't for everyone. But if you're up for it, what better occasion is there for all out drooling over a gorgeous physical specimen than a group of women (or men) celebrating a break up?

Another option is to simply hire a few handsome waiter types who are willing to serve food and drink to your guests wearing no shirts, just white collars and bow ties. This can be very successful with an all-female crowd.

Comedian
If you live in an urban area, you might think about hiring a stand-up comedian. Try to find one who's into relationship humor. Chat with them prior to the event so they know the back-story to the divorce.

Fortune Teller
It's always fun to have a psychic at a party. And what better time to ruminate on the future and all its romantic possibilities than a Divorce Party?

Makeup Artist

Why not hire a makeup artist to come to the party and do everyone's makeup? This can be lots of fun as well as instructive. Or you can do something unusual like have someone do temporary tattoos or body jewels.

Photographer

Hire a photographer to capture some candid shots of your special event. Plan to include a beautiful group shot. This can be nice keepsake to remember the true friends who stepped forward at a time of need.

Party Games

It's a great idea to plan to have several party games. Make sure you have all the materials before the party begins. You don't want to be hunting around for props. Also think about the timing of the games. The more outrageous ones should be kept till late in the evening when alcohol has flowed and inhibitions are out of the window.

Dart Board

Set up a simple dartboard. Tack a photograph of the UNMENTIONABLE ONE and have your guests throw darts at him or her. The one who hits the bullseye wins a prize. You can also play this game with a picture of the ex's lawyer's face on the dartboard, particularly if the divorce negotiations have been gruesome.

Run the Wedding Video Backwards

This is fun if you have a copy of the wedding video. Rewind so that the entire ceremony plays from end to beginning. The ring will be taken off, the couple will go backwards down the aisle and the bride will be whisked off in her car back to her life alone before she got into this big friggin' mess. If you want to be extra dramatic, play some loud accompanying music like Wagner's Flight of the Valkyries.

Slingshot

Use the wedding garter as a slingshot. Set up tin cans on a wall with his photo pasted on the top one. Take turns seeing who can knock him flying.

The Rings

After a marriage is over, what happens to the rings? Most get put away in a drawer. How about a game where guests offer their own creative ideas on what to do with the wedding and/or engagement rings? Have a large poster board on a table with big colored marker pens. Invite everyone to add suggestions to the list. Start it off yourself with ideas like:

- Have the diamond ring made into a nose or ear ring
- Melt the wedding ring down and have it made it into a new piece of jewelry
- Bury the wedding ring in a deep dark hole – in a metal box guaranteed to keep evil sealed away forever

Ring Funeral

Another idea is to have a mock Ring Funeral like in the "Dead and Buried" theme party. Ceremoniously place the ring inside a small box and bury it. Afterwards, crank up the music and dance on the grave.

Ring Smashing Ceremony

A company in Japan is now offering divorcing couples a Divorce Ceremony in which the couple smash their wedding rings with a hammer.

All you need for your version is the wedding ring and a four-pound sledgehammer. Pass the hammer around and allow everyone to enjoy the catharsis of smashing the ring to smithereens. Make it into a ceremony if so inclined along with new vows like "to have and to hold anyone you damn well please!"

Burn the Wedding Dress
Burning objects is primitive and oh so satisfying. Make a statement by burning the wedding dress at your Divorce Party. Be careful however if people are drinking. Dresses are usually very flammable. Do in an outdoor pit, never indoors. You don't want to burn the house down.

Burn the Bridesmaids' Dresses
Finally everyone can get their real feelings about the bridesmaid dresses off their chests. Let them vent about what a ruthless dictator you were forcing them to wear those hideous peach satin gowns. Then take the diabolical dresses and let them burn!

Pin the Part on the Old Fart
This is like Pin the Tail on the Donkey, only your guests will be pinning the "part" on "the old fart", aka your ex.

Play-Dough Man
The great thing about men made out of play-dough is they are literally putty in your hands. Get a bunch of kids' play dough and let your guests make little men out of them. Then let them do whatever they like to them - pull their heads off, poke their eyes out and anything else that comes into their evil little minds.

Carve Cantaloupes
Provide a pile of cantaloupes as well as a bunch of black markers and box cutters. Let your guests carve their melons to look like the men in their lives. Then take them into the yard for a melon-tossing contest. Enjoy watching them splatter all over the concrete or grass. The one who throws it the furthest is the winner.

A variation on this is to get hold of a pile of fruitcakes. Most stores have loads to get rid of after Christmas. Then let your party guests toss the fruitcakes out of their lives.

Penis *Piñata*

You can buy a penis *piñata* which you can hang from a tree (or the ceiling if it's cold outside). Have a big stick on hand. Your guests take turns smacking the thing until it explodes and candy flies everywhere. A definite icebreaker. Penis *piñata*s can be bought at bachelorette.com.

Revenge

This game is simple but can be very entertaining. Your guests take turns communicating their revenge fantasies against any ex who has done them wrong – whether it be ex-husbands or ex-lovers. This is like the inverse of the group hug, a chance to vent in a sympathetic setting. Get the game going by saying: I am imagining (Jerry) tied to a tree, his head covered in honey, and the biggest army of ants ever seen advancing on him...

Living Alone

Go around the group and have each person offer up one advantage of living alone. Here are some examples if people get stuck for ideas.

- You can leave 3 bitten chocolates in the box
- You can sleep fully clothed if you like it
- You don't have to shave your legs (or armpits)
- There are no more smelly socks under the bed
- You can wear ugly but toasty flannel nightgowns
- You can wear big comfy high-waisted panties

The Marriage Game

Write the following funny quotations about marriage on little pieces of paper and put them in a bowl. Your guests simply hand the bowl around and each person reads one aloud. Here are some good ones:

Write the following funny quotations about marriage on little pieces of paper and put them in a bowl. Your guests simply hand the bowl around and each person reads one aloud. Here are some good ones:

> The only thing a husband gets you is a dining set.

> Marriage is a great institution. But I'm not ready for an institution. - Mae West

> A woman is like a tea bag. You never know how strong she is till she gets in hot water. - Eleanor Roosevelt

> Keep your eyes wide open before marriage, half shut afterwards. - Benjamin Franklin

> For a while we pondered whether to take a vacation or get a divorce. We decided that a trip to Bermuda is over in two weeks, but a divorce is something you always have. - Woody Allen

> If you want to sacrifice the admiration of many men for the criticism of one, go ahead and get married. - Katherine Hepburn

> Either you give up or go on. - Debbie Reynolds

> Men who have pierced ears are better prepared for marriage. They've experienced pain and they've bought jewelry.

> Breaking up is like being hit by a Mack Truck. If you live through it, you start looking carefully to the left and to the right.

> Sometimes being a bitch is all a woman has to hold on to. - Dolores Claiborne

My husband and I never considered divorce. Murder perhaps, but never divorce. - Dr. Joyce Brothers.

I never hated a man enough to give his diamonds back. - Zsa Zsa Gabor

Marriage is like a dull meal with the dessert at the beginning.

Marriage is really tough because you have to deal with feelings and lawyers. - Richard Pryor

Marriage is the most expensive way for the average man to get his laundry done. - Burt Reynolds

Marriage is like a bank account. You put it in, you take it out, you lose interest.

Marriage begins with a prince kissing an angel. It ends with a bald-headed man looking across the table at a fat woman.

Marriage means you promise to give someone half your money for the rest of your life and not sleep with anyone else.

Marriage is the only way in which you sleep with the enemy.

Marriage is forever. It's like cement.

When you're young, you think of marriage as a train you simply have to catch. You run and run until you've caught it, and then you sit back and look out the window and realize you're bored.

The majority of husbands remind me of an orangutan trying to play the violin.

Destroy Photos

If the breakup has been bitter and bloody, this might be a good time to get rid of any photos of him that are still around. Obliterating wedding photos can be a big crowd pleaser. If you have a fireplace, burn them. Or provide your guests with glue and nature magazines and have them cut off his head and replace it with animal heads.

Top Ten List

…of things you all secretly disliked about him or her. Go around the room and everyone take turns telling what they secretly disliked about the one who's gone. If you can, get hold of the kid's toy, Mr. Microphone.

Blind Dates

Everyone brings a photograph of a single friend who might be a good blind date for the party girl or guy. Each guest promises to set up the date to be delivered within the next six months.

Pick Up Line Rehearsal

Before long the party girl's going to be back out in the dating world again. As we all know, it's a jungle out there. And she'll once again be encountering all those annoying pick up lines. Get her ready by giving her a run down of some of the funniest lines around.

Write the following pickup lines on small pieces of paper and put them in a bowl. Go around the room and have everyone pick out a line and read it aloud.

- Your body's name must be Visa, because it's everywhere I want to be.
- Can I buy you a drink, or do you just want the money?
- I may not be Fred Flintstone, but I bet I can make your bed rock.
- I may not be the best looking guy here, but I'm the only one talking to you.
- Yo Baby, you be my Dairy Queen, I'll be your Burger King, you treat me right, and I'll do it your way.

- Excuse me, do you have your phone number, I seem to have lost mine.
- I can't find my puppy, can you help me find him? I think he went into this cheap motel room.
- I'm new in town. Could I have directions to your house?
- If you were a new hamburger at McDonald's, you would be McGorgeous.
- You might not be the best looking girl here, but beauty is only a light switch away.
- That's a nice shirt. Can I talk you out of it?
- There must be something wrong with my eyes, I can't take them off you.
- Are you from Tennessee? Because you're the only ten I see!
- Was your father a thief? 'Cause someone stole the stars from the sky and put them in your eyes.
- Your daddy must have been a baker, 'cause you've got a nice set of buns.
- Do you have a map? I just keep on getting lost in your eyes.
- Excuse me, I lost my teddy bear - will you sleep with me tonight?
- He: Can I borrow your phone?
  She: Why?
  He: So I can call my mom and tell her I just met the girl of my dreams.
- Are your pants from outer space? 'Cause your butt is out of this world.
- Are you a parking ticket? 'Cause you got fine-fine-fine written all over ya.
- He: I can't wait until tomorrow.
  She: Why not?
  He: Because you look better every day.
- Are you tired? Because you've been running through my mind all day!
- If I could rearrange the alphabet I'd put U and I together!
- I must be in heaven cause I've seen an angel.

- He: (while peeking at label inside the neck of a shirt or dress) Just checking to see if it's true.
  She: What?
  He: That you're made in heaven.

Laugh Till It Hurts

So you haven't been able to spring for a comedian. Choose the best joke teller in the group and have them perform for the crowd by reading divorce jokes aloud. Here are a few favorites:

> Getting married is very much like going to a restaurant with friends. You order what you want, then when you see what the other person has, you wish you had ordered that.

> At the cocktail party, one woman said to another, "Aren't you wearing your wedding ring on the wrong finger?"
> The other replied, "Yes, I am, I married the wrong man."

> After a quarrel, a husband said to his wife, "You know, I was a fool when I married you."
> She replied, "Yes, dear, but I was in love and didn't notice."

> A woman inserted an 'ad' in the classifieds: "Husband wanted." Next day she received a hundred letters. They all said the same thing: "You can have mine."

> The bride, upon her engagement, went to her mother and said, "I've found a man just like father!"
> Her mother replied, "So what do you want from me, sympathy?"

> When a woman steals your husband, there is no better revenge than to let her keep him.

Sixty percent of married men cheat in America. The rest cheat in Europe.

Man is incomplete until he is married. Then he is finished.

A little boy asked his father, "Daddy, how much does it cost to get married?"
And the father replied, "I don't know yet son, I'm still paying."

A woman was telling her friend, "It is I who made my husband a millionaire." "And what was he before you married him?" asked the friend. The woman replied, "A billionaire."

Marriage is the triumph of imagination over intelligence. A second marriage is the triumph of hope over experience.

Just think, if it weren't for marriage, men would go through life thinking they had no faults at all.

You know the honeymoon is pretty much over when you start to go out with the boys on Wednesday nights, and so does she.

First guy (proudly): "My wife's an angel!" Second guy: "You're lucky, mine's still alive."

Why don't women blink during foreplay?
They don't have time.

Why does it take 1 million sperm to fertilize one egg?
They won't stop to ask directions.

What do men and sperm have in common?

They both have a one-in-a-million chance of becoming a human being.

What is the difference between men and government bonds?
The bonds mature.

Why are blonde jokes so short?
So men can remember them.

Why is it difficult to find men who are sensitive, caring and good looking?
They all already have boyfriends.

What are a woman's four favorite animals?
A mink in the closet, a Jaguar in the garage, a tiger in the bedroom, and an ass to pay for it all.

Why are married women heavier than single women?
Single women come home, see what's in the fridge and go to bed.
Married women come home, see what's in bed and go to the fridge.

How did Pinocchio find out he was made of wood?
His hand caught fire.
What did God say after creating man?
I must be able to do better than that.

What did God say after creating Eve?
"Practice makes perfect."

How are men and parking spots alike?
Good ones are always taken.
Free ones are mostly handicapped or extremely small.

Ever notice how many of women's problems can be traced to the male gender?
MENstruation
MENopause
MENtal breakdown
GUYnecology
HIMmorrhoids

Why do men like BMWs?
They can spell it.

What do an anniversary and a toilet have in common?
Men always miss them.

Ten Things You'll Never Hear a Man Say:
10. Here honey, you use the remote.
 9. You know, I'd like to see her again, but her breasts are just too big.
 8. Ooh, Antonio Banderas AND Brad Pitt? That's one movie I gotta see!
 7. While I'm up, can I get you anything?
 6. Honey since we don't have anything else planned, will you go to the wallpaper store with me?
 5. Sex isn't that important; sometimes, I just want to be held.
 4. Why don't you go to the mall with me and help me pick out a pair of shoes?
 3. Aww, forget Monday night football, Let's watch Melrose Place.
 2. Hey let me hold your purse while you try that on.
 1. We never talk anymore.

Why E-Mail is Like a Male Reproductive Organ:
10. Those who have it would be devastated if it were ever cut off.

9. Those who have it think that those who don't are somehow made to feel inferior.
8. Those who don't have it may agree that it's neat, but think it's not worth the fuss that those who have it make about it.
7. Many of those who don't have it would like to try it (e-mail envy).
6. It's more fun when it's up, but this makes it hard to get any real work done.
5. In the distant past, its only purpose was to transmit information vital to the survival of the species. Some people still think that's the only thing it should be used for, but most folks today use it for fun most of the time.
4. If you don't apply the appropriate measures, it can spread viruses.
3. If you use it too much, you'll find it becomes more and more difficult to think coherently.
2. We attach an importance to it that is far greater than its actual size and influence warrant.
1. If you're not careful what you do with it, it can get you into a lot of trouble.

Adam was walking around the Garden of Eden feeling very lonely. So God asked Adam, "What is wrong?" Adam said he didn't have anyone with whom to talk.

God said he was going to give him a companion and it would be a woman. He said, this person will cook for you and wash your clothes and she will always agree with every decision you make. She will bear you children and never ask you to get up in the middle of the night to take care of them. She will not nag you, and will always be the first to admit she was wrong when you have had a disagreement. She will never have a headache, and will freely give you love and compassion whenever needed.

Adam asked God, "What would a woman like this cost?" God said, "An arm and a leg." Adam said "What can I get for just a rib?"

The rest is history.

Chapter Seven
Divorce Party Music

It's very important to select music that will create the right mood. Choose music that's fun. Avoid anything sappy, serious or sentimental. Select songs that treat love and loss with a good dose of humor or a nice helping of irony. Do not under any circumstances play "their" favorite song. In fact, make of point of smashing that CD to pieces. (Or take it outside and have one of the guests run over it with their car.)

If you can, hire a DJ. You can probably find one who will play music with a breakup theme. If you can't afford a DJ, appoint one guest to be in charge of the music. He or she can provide the right punctuation for the evening with a well-chosen song. For example, an excellent arriving song is Gloria Gaynor's "I Will Survive".

You might also look into renting a karaoke machine for the night. It will provide some excellent entertainment and if you live in a large urban area you might be able to find one that will offer a package of breakup songs that everyone will enjoy.

You might want to shift the mood at some point with a good balance of funny breakup songs and rousing party music. You can even give a taped compilation of the party songs as party favors.

Break-Up Song List
I Can See Clearly Now – Johnny Nash
D-I-V-O-R-C-E - Tammy Wynette
Hit The Road Jack - Ray Charles
One More Kiss Dear - Vangelis
Burnin' Down the House – Talking Heads

Na Na Hey Hey Kiss Him Goodbye - Steam
I Will Survive - Gloria Gaynor
50 Ways to Leave Your Lover - Paul Simon
I Can See Clearly Now - Jimmy Cliff/ Gladys Knight and the Pips
We Are Family – Sister Sledge
Who's Sorry Now - Connie Francis
"Respect" - Aretha Franklin
You'll Never Find Another Love Like Mine - Lou Rawls
Goodbye To You - Scandal
Why Do Fools Fall In Love - Frankie Lymond
She Got The Goldmine I Got The Shaft - Jerry Reed
Have A Nice Rest Of Your Life – Randy Travis
Nookie - Limp Bizkit
We Are the Champions - Queen
The Best is Yet to Come - Frank Sinatra
I'm Coming Out - Diana Ross
Kiss My Ass - Ted Nugent
Lies - Knickerbocker
Life Goes on - LeAnne Rymes
Living in a House Divided - Cher
Love Stinks - J. Geils Band
Love Don't Live Here Anymore - Madonna
Mr. Lonely - Bobby Vinton
My Heart Will Go On - Celine Dion
Needles and Pins - The Seekers
Never Be Your Fool Again - Deanna Cox
Off and Running - Leslie Gore
Party Time - T.G. Sheppard
People are Strange - The Doors
I Beg Your Pardon (I never promised you a rose garden) – Lynn Anderson
You're Breaking My Heart – Harry Nilsson

Generic Rousing Party Songs
Let's Dance – David Bowie
One Love, Jamming – Bob Marley
Good Day Sunshine – The Beatles
Girls Just Want to Have Fun, True Colors – Cyndi Lauper
Lola, You Really Got Me – The Kinks
Honky Tonk Woman, Brown Sugar, Jumpin' Jack Flash – Rolling Stones
Love Shack – B52s
Glory Days – Bruce Springsteen
Every Breath You Take – Police
Little Red Corvette, 1999, Purple Rain – Prince
Like a Virgin, Papa Don't Preach – Madonna
Signed, Sealed, Delivered – Stevie Wonder
Do You Really Want to Hurt Me – Culture Club
What's Love Got to Do With It, Proud Mary – Tina Turner
Billie Jean, Thriller – Michael Jackson
Slow Hand – Pointer Sisters

Chapter Eight
Perfect Prizes and Decorations

This is a night to remember so don't skimp on your party decorations. You want your guests to walk into the party and immediately get the tone of the event. Decorations can be purchased at party stores or you can make them yourself. Be creative as you devise offbeat ways of decorating the party space.

Torn Photographs
If the sight of the ex doesn't make the party girl or guy throw up, consider hanging lots of photos of the once happy couple torn in half. Use paper clips or clothes pins to dangle the photos on colored yarn stretched across the rooms.

Banners
You can proclaim your party theme with a custom banner hung across the room or even outside. Check online for party banner companies like party411.com to order custom banners. U.K. party throwers can buy a terrific 18ft. long banner that reads, "Delighted to be Divorced". This is available from partybox.co.uk.

Another idea is to create a banner with an acronym, such as:

Delighted
Inspired
Victorious
Optimistic

Raring to Go
Confident
Energized

Free
Raring to go!
Excited
Ecstatic
Divorced!
On my own – at last!
Motivated

Caricatures
Many party companies will create a caricature if you provide a photo of the ex. The caricature can be used to make cutouts, centerpieces, even invitations. Provide guests with markers for graffiti.

Paper or Fabric Garlands
You can also buy lots of shiny colored paper garlands to add to the festivity. Or visit a fabric shop and buy long swathes of filmy material to drape on the ceiling. Make sure there are no candles or flames close by.

Life Size Cutouts
Imagine walking into the party and finding a custom life size cutout of the ex positioned by the entrance. You could even have a balloon coming out of his/her mouth saying: "Harumph! I'm not invited". Or you can have the ex's face superimposed on a life-size witch, Dracula or Frankenstein. Again, give your guests free rein (and markers) to "comment" on the departed one.

Funny Quotes
Another idea is to write a slew of funny quotations on big cards and hang them around the room. Here are a few examples:

An ex-spouse is like an inflamed appendix...they cause a lot of pain and suffering, but after they're removed...you find out you didn't really need them anyway.

Ginger Rogers did everything Fred Astaire did, but she did it backwards and in high heels.

I have yet to hear a man ask for advice on how to combine marriage and a career.

So many men, so few who can afford me.

Coffee, chocolate, men...some things are just better rich.

Don't treat me any differently than you would a queen.

Warning: I have an attitude and I know how to use it.

Balloons

An easy decorating solution is to simply order balloons just like you would for an engagement or wedding party. Have them printed with your party theme, the name of the party girl or guy, or "Congratulations On Your Divorce!" A combination of pink and black balloons is always very effective.

Flowers

If you decide to have flowers at the party, try to match them with your party theme. Bear in mind the associations people attach to specific flowers. For example, avoid romantic flowers like roses which symbolize love. And definitely avoid stephanotis which symbolizes marital happiness...peonies which connote bashfulness...or hydrangeas connoting heartlessness. One punk bride we know chose black roses and dead bouquets for her Divorce Party.

If the party girl has a great sense of humor, and if the person who caught the bouquet at the original wedding is present, consider having a little ceremony where the bouquet recipient ceremoniously tosses a small bouquet back to the ex-bride as a gesture expressing that she's free to move on and find true love again.

Recommended Flowers for a Divorce Party:

- Tulips for love, fame and passion
- Orchids for love and beauty
- Lilies for happiness, honor, truth and purity
- Larkspur for laughter

Do-It-Yourself Centerpieces

You may decide to have one or two centerpieces if your food is being served buffet-style. You may need more if you are having a sit down meal. Either way, you can make very effective centerpieces without a lot of work. Here are a few simple ideas.

- Fill a glass cylinder vase with whole or sliced lemons. After all, sometimes you get a lemon…then you have to divorce it.

- Do the same thing with the lemons then wedge in a big beautiful flower like a vibrant Gerber daisy. The symbolism is obvious.

- Fill little bud vases with sprigs of different herbs. Put little cards next to them with their traditional connotations. Parsley = new beginnings. Mint = wisdom. Thyme = courage.

- Have a single flower like a colorful open poppy with a card announcing the divorced person's new single status.

- Buy some beautiful big apples. Cut a little wedge out of each apple's top for a votive candle.

Lighting

Good lighting cannot be overemphasized. You do not want harsh unflattering light at a time like this. You can't go wrong with lots and lots of light strings. These create a festive and flattering light, very important for anyone emerging from a bad relationship.

Disco Ball
Is there room for dancing? Then hang a disco ball. These are fun and can be rented from most party supply companies. Or you can purchase one quite cheaply through party catalogs like Oriental Trading Company.

Guest Book
A Guest Book is a nice way to remember all the great folks who turned out for this event. You can have a traditional sign in board or book (available from party411.com). Or you can do something like have a big blowup photo of the bride and groom torn in half which guests can sign with a black marker and even add choice comments. Another nice idea is a keepsake pewter tray which the party guests can sign. This is available from signaturesremembered.com.

Prizes and Party Favors
Be sure you have prizes for your party games as well as party favors for your guests to take home. Party favors are a nice way of thanking your guests for coming and work well if they tie in with the party theme. Here are some offbeat ideas:

"Men are such fools" candles
- Forget Him tea bags
- Voodoo doll
- "Wash away your sins" soap - amazon.com
- Custom candy bar wrappers with photo or personalized inscription. (They slip easily onto regular size candy bars). – www.party411.com
- Floral special memories one-use cameras – guests can take their own pictures and have lasting memories. – www.wholesalefavors.com

Bumper Stickers

A nice turn of phrase on a bumper sticker is a great memento of the party. You can buy lots of fun stickers or have your own made up for the occasion. Here are some favorites:

Who knew forever would mean a year?
My lawyer can beat up your lawyer.
I got the Porsche...He got the cocktail waitress.
He got the girlfriend. I got the house, the car, and the Visa card.
Marriage is grand. Divorce is 100 grand.
Some call it love and marriage. I call it bait and switch.
Marriage is an institution...I'm not ready for an institution.
A man is incomplete until he gets married. Then he's finished.
The shortest sentence is "I am". The longest sentence is "I do".
Divorce...the Ultimate Weight Loss Plan
Check out Party411.com and Stickergiant.com for more ideas.

Fridge Magnets

Fridge magnets make great favors, especially if they tie in with the party theme. There are loads available online or you can custom design your own. For example:

The first two husbands are just for practice.
I think you're mistaking me for someone you want me to be.
Fuck this fifties housewife bullshit.
Ran into my ex. Then backed up and ran over him again.
When I married Mr. Right I didn't know his first name was Always.
All are available from Party411.com

Votive Candles

The lighting of candles has always signified respect and remembrance. Let your guests remember the great time they had at your Divorce Party with a reusable votive candle. While votives are usually sold as bridal shower favors, you can add your own personalized twist. For example, "Gina and Jeremy...Not!"

Custom votives (playing cards and more) are available at customwedding.com.

Divorce Party Toilet Paper
A nice touch and one your guests will enjoy is to stock the bathroom with Ex-wife or Ex-husband toilet paper. This most excellent item can be purchased at chocolatefantasies.com.

Chapter Nine
Buy, Borrow and Rent

Depending on your budget, you need to decide what to buy, borrow or rent as you gather your party supplies. You may have to improvise some items. For example, it's not likely you'll be able to go to a party shop and find a section offering Divorce Party tableware, though the trend is growing. Silver or gold paper plates and tablecloths are always a party pleaser. You might personalize them by ordering matching cocktail napkins with something written on them like "Sally Smith, Single and Available". Or you might order one of the bachelorette party kits (napkins, plates, cups). Recommended is the "devil girl" kit, the "no men? Amen!" kit or the "imaginary men" kit, all available from plumparty.com.

Checklist of Supplies and Equipment:
Chairs
Tables
Lights
Speakers
Plates
Utensils
Napkins
Tablecloths
Glasses
Chafing dishes (for hot food)
Trash cans
Decorations
Flowers

Centerpieces
Food
Cake
Drinks
Ice
Candles
Party favors
Prizes
Disposable cameras
Place cards

Chapter Ten
Last Minute Preparations

You wake up in the morning and it hits you. Tonight is the Divorce Party! There are several things to take care of today that will guarantee the party goes smoothly.

If Your Party is in a Rented Space

- Call and confirm the reservation.
- Double check start and finish time.
- Alert the venue of any deliveries e.g. a cake.
- Confirm your DJ.
- If you're doing your own music, pack the CDs.
- Confirm your caterer.
- Confirm all liquor is being delivered.

If Your Party is in a Private Home

During the day you will need to set up the party space, check that you have everything you need, and make sure any helpers know exactly what they're doing.

Preparing A Home for a Party

A few preparations will add to guest convenience and ensure safety:

- Put away any breakables.
- Roll up slippery rugs.
- Put markers on any glass doors. (Any stickers will work).

- Arrange the kitchen to discourage guests from hanging out near hot stoves.
- Put plenty of guest towels and extra toilet paper in the bathroom.
- Put up signs pointing to the bathroom so you won't be spending the whole evening telling people where it is.
- Also, put a sign up at the entrance indicating where people should put their coats.

Check Supplies and Equipment

Double check you have everything you need using the checklist in Chapter 9.

Remember to have tips ready for any hired staff.

Arrange the Party Space

The key to a good use of party space is to spread out tables, chairs and other activity areas so that congestion is minimized and guests are free to move around and mingle. Food and drink should be well away from doors or dance spaces because these will be busy areas. And think through where to have any party games or entertainment so that the party will flow smoothly.

If there is any kind of a ceremony like the Unwedding, set out chairs in rows, allowing 3 feet from the edge of one chair to the back of the next. And make the aisle space twice the width of the people who will walk down it.

Prepare Divorce Shower Gift Unwrapping Ceremony

You will need:

- A prominent chair for the unmarried one.
- A writing pad and pen for the gift/giver list.
- A sturdy paper plate and scissors for the shower bouquet. (Bows and ribbons are threaded through the plate.)
- A trash bag for the wrapping paper.
- A camera.

Set up the bar

The bar should be set up away from the main activity but not too far so as to be inconvenient. If indoors, choose an area with plenty of room so there is no crush. If outdoors, find a location that is safe, shady and convenient.

When setting up the bar area, make sure you have plenty of whatever you need to make the cocktails or other drinks you are serving. Be sure that any wines will be ready to serve at the correct temperature. Only white wine needs to be chilled. And don't forget to chill the nonalcoholic beverages and waters.

Finally, put out as many glasses as you have room for. Keep the rest in the kitchen for now. And don't forget to double check that you have all the other bar supplies on your list.

Setting up a buffet

Most party food is served buffet style. The food is laid out on tables from which guests help themselves. The food is usually finger friendly since buffets are eaten standing up or with plates in laps.

Take the time to think through how the food will be arranged on the buffet table. Use post-it notes to position where the dishes will sit. You won't have to think about any of it once the party begins.

With a buffet, you can have a lavish centerpiece to dress up the table. And make sure the buffet is navigable. If possible, set the table up so guests can serve from both sides. At the starting end of the table, place a stack of plates and have the utensils rolled into napkins so they can be easily carried. Keep it simple according to the food served. Usually a fork and spoon will suffice. Put some at the beginning of the table and some at the end. And make sure there are enough plates and utensils set out for guests who go back for seconds.

Now arrange the platters, bowls and dishes so that the food presents in a logical fashion. Hot foods can be in chafing dishes which come equipped with heating candles to keep the food warm. Cold food dishes can be nestled in bowls of ice which help keep the food chilled and fresh.

To make it look attractive, display the dishes at different levels. Simply place pans or bowls upside down on the table, drape them with a tablecloth or napkin and place the bowls or platters on top.

Make sure the serving trays or bowls are small enough so they can be easily carried out and refilled in the kitchen. Buffet guests tend to eat more, particularly if they are consuming alcohol at the same time.

Sit Down Meals

If you are doing a sit down meal, make sure you set the tables properly before anyone arrives. Have Place Cards so that guests are arranged for a good mix. And make sure everyone has easy access to bread and condiments.

Designate!

Remember, if you're throwing the party, don't take on all the work on the night itself. You'll go crazy. You'll be exhausted. And you won't enjoy yourself. Ask friends beforehand if they will take on a job like filling up the ice bucket or watching the table and restocking the food. Someone has to be responsible for picking up used plates and glasses. A lot of clutter tends to indicate a party is over before it really is.

Plan the Activities

A good party seems to move along with its own momentum. But if you're having games or entertainment, make sure you think through your sequence ahead of time. And make sure any supplies are close at hand. You don't want to waste time or lose your group's interest by hunting around for props or prizes.

Also, keep anything too raucous or outrageous for later in the evening when the alcohol has flowed and inhibitions are out of the window. And be prepared for tears and outpourings of emotion. Remember, underneath all the hilarity are real feelings and real suffering. This is a great time to get it out once and for all. Be sure to have plenty of tissues on hand for spontaneous weeping.

Chapter Eleven
Let's Party

Guests Arrive

Make sure someone greets the guests and lets them know where to put their belongings and get a drink. This will help the party kick off smoothly and get everyone on the same wavelength. It's important to set the tone and make guests feel instantly comfortable. Remember this may be their very first Divorce Party!

Keep the Party Flowing

As the party host, you're the steady beacon in the midst of all the chaos and excitement. It's up to you to keep the party moving. No special experience is required for this role. It all comes down to creativity and staying attuned to the social atmosphere. You can feel when people are enjoying what they are doing in which case take your time moving on to the next activity. But if you feel like the energy level is dwindling, be ready to switch gears. You don't want any of those horrible social silences where people start to glance at watches and think: What am I doing here? It all comes down to good preparations. Be ready for anything! And most of all, have a wonderful time!

Chapter Twelve
Funny Party Themes

Sometimes the events surrounding a divorce can be so painful or horrible that laughter is the only way of holding back the tears. The following parties are definitely for those in the mood to laugh.

Survivor Party
The theme says it all—he or she survived. Hooray! Party guests come dressed as desert island survivors celebrating a lucky escape from the sinking ship of marriage.

For your invitations, use a beach motif. You might also pick up some travel brochures from a travel agency and slip the invitation inside before mailing. As for dress attire, think of the gritty sexy TV Survivor look. Bikini tops and sarongs or shorts accessorized with bandanas, sunglasses, and ankle bracelets.

Outside hang a banner which reads: "Life's A Beach". Have the party anthem "I Will Survive" blasting as people arrive. Have copies of the words scattered around so guests can join in at full throttle. Furnish the party space with borrowed beach chairs, umbrellas and hammocks. If the party is indoors in the winter, turn up the heat to simulate the tropics. And have tropical fans blowing to cool people down.

You could also set up a tanning room where fake tan is sprayed on the guests. If there is a pool available, swimming might be nice. Have the guests float around on airbeds sipping cocktails supplied by waiters dressed as island natives or Robinson Crusoe.

A fun game is to have a supply of "Wilson" basketballs on hand. Set out colored markers and have guests compete, like Tom Hanks in the movie "Cast Away", to make up the most original Wilson ball with a prize given at the end of the night.

For party food, think desert island cuisine. If you want to splurge, spring for fresh crab. You might even fill the bathtub with live crabs – guests have to select a crab, then drop it themselves into big pots of boiling water. Remind them to drop the crabs in head first – it's more humane. Sushi is another possibility. You could even hire a sushi chef to make up tasty little morsels. Ask the staff at a local sushi joint if they moonlight.

Pineapples and coconuts are a must, at the very least as decoration. You could also make sure your bartender is skilled in cutting them up and using the fresh pineapple or coconut milk to make yummy fresh cocktails like Pina Coladas served in coconut shells, or Mai Tais, with little paper umbrellas of course. The perfect custom cocktail for this party is The Lifeboat.

Party favors might be inflatable pool floaters, spritz bottles or mini personal blow fans. If your party's all women, consider coconut bras which are available at orientaltradingcompany.com.

Lemon Party

The theme here of course is "if life gives you lemons, make lemonade", the perfect aphorism for the newly divorced person. The flip side of course is: "congratulations on getting rid of your lemon".

Design the invitations with a lemon graphic. Or buy designer lemon note cards (available from healingbaskets.com). Ask your guests to wear yellow. Gifts should be anything lemon... from soaps and shampoos to a lemon squeezer to lemon candles to lemon drops to homemade lemon curd. For decorations, buy strings of lemon-shaped party lights. Hang a banner stating: "When life gives you lemons, make lemonade" or "Don't get stuck with a lemon (if you do, squeeze it dry)".

Food should be lemon-themed. For example, cold poached salmon with lemon wedges served with green salad with lemon poppy seed dressing. For dessert, have lemon tart or lemon meringue pie or lemon bars. Make up plenty of homemade lemonade, though be sure to have tequila or vodka or gin on hand to spice this up.

Party favors complete the lemon theme. You could give gift baskets of fresh lemons or even little fledgling lemon trees. Or you could give everyone a nice pair of lemon colored slipper socks for those cozy nights at home. (Available from healingbaskets.com.)

Lemonade
Lemon Juice, freshly squeezed from 8 large lemons (1-1/2 cups)
1/2 cup of sugar, granulated
5 cups cold water
1 large lemon, cut into small wedges or thin cartwheel slices
Freshly made ice cubes.
In a large pitcher, combine the freshly squeezed lemon juice, sugar and 2 cups of cold water. Stir briskly to dissolve the sugar. Add the remaining ingredients and stir briskly again.

The UnWedding
The UnWedding is basically a wedding in reverse. It can be an elaborate affair. Or it can be a casual event in a friend's backyard.

For example, the unbride might choose to wear her wedding gown. She might come down the "aisle" between the seated guests to undo her vows and regain her single status. She might officially reclaim her maiden name, or do something symbolic and dramatic like take off her white gown to reveal a red body leotard or sequined red evening dress underneath.

At the reception she may cut an unwedding cake topped by a confident, happy, independent woman. She might smear it mischievously all over her own face.

A bridesmaid may toss the bouquet so the unbride catches it. The wedding video may be played in reverse so the bride and groom walk backwards out of the ceremony to their separate lives.

Party favor ideas for the unwedding can be anything that's a twist on a traditional wedding favor. For example, those little bags of sugar almonds with a nice card "Celebrate our divorce" or..."Watch out for the nuts".

Coming Out Party

This party is a new twist on a debutante party, because this event is the coming out of a newly single person. The divorcee is being launched into the community with a whole new status.

If the budget allows it, consider doing this party at a swanky old hotel like the Biltmore in Los Angeles or the Ritz in New York. Dress is formal, preferably evening gowns. The Coming Out Party is a great excuse to dress to the nines complete with gloves and fans if desired. Hire a videographer to capture the party especially the moment when the party girl makes a dramatic entrance, hopefully down a sweeping staircase. Okay, you can slide down the banister if you prefer. It's your party so anything goes.

Inviting lots of eligible partners to this party is a definite plus. Encourage them to give the one coming out lots of attention. Major flirting is in order.

The dinner should of course be a sit-down elegant affair. If held in a hotel, reserve a private room if the budget allows.

Inner Bitch Party

This party can be lots of fun and is definitely for the all-female crowd, particularly if emotions are running hot. Have guests dress tough – leather is good. As guests arrive, you might hand out "Bitch" t-shirts (available at cafepress.com) or "Heartless Bitch" t-shirts (available at HeartlessBitches.com).

Decorate the space with bitch slogans written on posters.

Examples:
5% angel, 95% bitch.
I bitch, therefore I am.
Auntie Em: Hate you, hate Kansas, taking the dog – Dorothy.
Caution: I can go from 0 to bitch in 2.5 seconds.
I don't suffer from insanity – I enjoy every minute of it.

I used to have an open mind but my brains kept falling out.
I used to think I was indecisive, but now I'm not too sure.
I want to be just like Barbie. That Bitch has everything!
I wasn't born a bitch. Men like you made me that way.
It's as BAD as you think, and they ARE out to get you.
It's Been Lovely But I Have To Scream Now.
My other car is a broom.
Next mood swing: 6 minutes.

The order of the day for food is tough and hot. This can include any kind of red meat, hot sauces, salsas. Carne asada would be perfect.

Party favors might be Elizabeth Hilts' book: "Getting In Touch With Your Inner Bitch" which rails against "toxic niceness" and advocates the mantra, "I don't think so!"

Freedom Party

This bash celebrates liberation, whether it be from a bad relationship or from the life-draining bad times that followed the breakup. The party theme is built on breaking out. Guests might be given prison stripe t-shirts on arrival which can be thrown off once the party is in top gear. Food and drink is abundant and decadent befitting the palate of the long deprived prisoner of love. Consider renting a karaoke machine so that guests can truly let it all out.

Order a great divorce cake topped with something fitting like a woman free and alone, driving a pink convertible. For party favors and game prizes, get handcuffs (they might be useful later) and tiny balls and chains. Or buy a bunch of Alcatraz t-shirts. Available from cafepress.com.

Punch Party

Bottling up negative emotion like anger has long been believed to cause emotional and even physical problems. Sadly, anger and divorce often go hand in hand. An easy and fun way to release pent up anger or frustration is to have a Punch Bag Party.

Ask your guests to come dressed in workout clothes. Rig up the party space with several punching bags. Before letting your guests loose to attack the bags, it's a good idea to have someone give them some basic boxing techniques. For example:

- When throwing a punch, keep muscles loose and snap punches out.
- Keep your power at the end of your punches by making sure that your arm is fully extended when your fist strikes the bag.
- Try to always hit the bag with your hand knuckles, not your finger knuckles.
- And maintain balance by staying on the balls of your feet at all times.

For best results, demonstrate first yourself. This can be especially satisfying if it's your Divorce Party. Be sure to vent consciously as you punch. Focus yourself on who or what you're angry with, whether it's the ex or someone who came between you. Feel free to fantasize heavily. Attach a photograph if it helps. Imagine every punch to hit the source of your troubles square on the kisser. Pummel mercilessly till they're on their knees begging. If nothing else, the good physical workout will leave you feeling energized and refreshed.

Punching bags can be found in most sports equipment stores or online. But you can also make your own.

HOW TO MAKE A PUNCHING BAG:

1. Cut a leg off an old pair of jeans. Sew or glue the bottom of the leg closed.
2. Stuff the leg with a soft pillow. For more resistance, stuff with styrofoam peanuts, marbles or uncooked beans.
3. Consider stuffing your bag with physical evidence of whatever's been bothering you of late. If your relationship is still

causing you aggravation, cram it with photos, clothes, court documents or other mementos.
4. Tie one end with a cord and hang it from the ceiling.
5. Punch, kick, elbow or head butt to your heart's content.

For those gentle souls who balk at punching anything, you can offer a secondary activity that is less aggressive and more p.c. such as stomping bubble wrap. Buy sheets of it from a packing store and lay them out on the floor of a room. Invite your guests to stomp to their heart's content. This might sound silly, but it's actually very addictive. There are even websites for virtual stomping like www.virtualbubblewrap.com.

Drinks can be punch, especially our elegant punch recipe. (See p.25.) Food might be muscle-building foods like an athlete would eat, such as red meats, pastas and cheeses.

Voodoo Party

A voodoo party can be lots of fun and also cathartic. Any residual bad feelings can be expended once and for all. The party space should be decorated in silver and black.

Besides the obvious sticking of pins into voodoo dolls, another perfect activity for the Voodoo Party might be to toss any of the ex's belongings into a fire. Burning personal items like left behind underwear or socks can be immensely satisfying, bringing out the primitive in the best of us. Some party throwers even take photographs of the items being consumed by flames to send to the ex later or to stick in the family album.

Other evil things you might do at your voodoo party? Use his cherished Callaway golf club as a spit to roast chickens on the outdoor barbecue. Pass around those naked pictures you took of your ex on the honeymoon. Have a guest call your ex on the phone to say they've just won a brand new Porsche. Log onto that dating site you know he hangs out on every night and have your guests shower him with flattering instant messages.

Fun party favors can be Nunzillas, little wind-up Nun dolls that spit sparks, available from officeplaygroundcom. Or a book of voodoo spells such as "Doctor Snake's Voodoo Spell Book", available from amazon.com.

Lazerzone (or Paintball) Party
Laserzone arcades are not just for children. Most weekends you can find grownups at these fun places, celebrating 40th. birthdays, engagements and yes, even divorce parties. Having your event at a place already set up for parties has many practical advantages. They provide you with readymade invitations. And you simply show up at the allotted time with your friends. At Laserzone you blast each other with laser guns as you run around a course lit with glowing black light. This can be a great way to expend any aggressive energy especially if you invite males and females and make it a battle of the sexes. Afterwards you go into your own private party room to feed on pizza and cake or whatever you want. This party is highly recommended and lots of fun.

A Paintball Party can be equally satisfying. A fun idea would be to have one team have masks made from a photo of the ex and the goal is to wipe them off the face of the earth. Another nice way of expelling aggression.

Dead and Buried
Warning! This party is not for everyone. It's tailor-made for punky partygoers or those with the sickest senses of humor. The theme revolves around the death of the relationship.

Guests come dressed for a funeral, all in black. The party space is decorated with dead flowers. You might even spring for a funeral wreath with the couple's name in the center.

The event kicks off with the official placing of the wedding ring into a funeral urn. You can make your own funeral urn using a small box. A tooth fairy box would work. Or you can buy a real one. Funeral directors sell them, but they're usually marked up. It's best to buy one online from companies like CremationUrnFactory.com. Costco also sells mail order urns.

Of course, if the ring is valuable, seriously think about using a symbolic drugstore ring. While you might just want to be rid of the wretched ring, in a few months you'll be kicking yourself for not selling it and using the money for that Macy's sale or a much-needed vacation.

The ring/urn is ceremoniously placed into a deep dark hole. Guests help toss in soil, banishing it to darkness for all eternity. Consider erecting a small gravestone with the couple's married name and, of course, R.I.P. On the other hand, if the union was particularly gruesome, treat it like a pauper's grave and leave it unmarked and uncared for, lost in the blizzard of time.

Then, after the macabre part is over, like with all good funerals, it's time to party! Let it all hang out. And don't look back.

The Scene of the Crime

This party is also not for the faint of heart. It takes place at the scene of the crime, the place where the marriage vows were sealed or the fateful marriage proposal was uttered.

This party could easily be blended with The Unwedding. Or you could make a very entertaining evening by hiring one of those actor troupes who stage a mystery which your guests have to unravel. After all, love is a mystery. Who knows why it sometimes flourishes and sometimes fades?

If you have a particularly dark sense of humor, you could rig it so that the murderer ends up being your ex who can be discovered hiding (in cardboard cutout form), murder weapon in hand.

For those who prefer more sedate entertainment, just have the board game Clue set up at a table.

Trash the Dress

Trashing the dress has become a trend for photographers to document in the aftermath of some weddings. It's also a great theme for a Divorce Party and a great way to get rid of that morbid object handing like a ghost in your closet. You might invite guests to bring their own old unwanted wedding dresses to the party to add to the fun.

How to trash the dress? Let your imagination go wild. You can roll the dress in mud. You can run over it with cars. You can hang it up and let the guests go it with spray paint, or knives, or blowtorches. Plan ahead and have any props and tools set up and ready.

Kevin Cotter has a humorous website and book on this topic. He began by fantasizing what to do with his ex wife's wedding dress. This turned into an elaborate rumination on possible uses for the dress likre using it as a shower curtain, a tow rope or a sunshade for a car windshield.

Chapter Thirteen
Sexy Party Themes

If the party girl or guy is well on the road to recovery and definitely ready to go out into the dating world again, you might consider having a sexy Divorce Party. This party reaffirms the power and pleasure of sex. Even better, the party can remind divorcees that sex can be playful and fun, something that's probably a distant memory for one coming out of a dead marriage.

Hot, Hot, Hot!
This Divorce Party was held in Los Angeles' infamous Laurel Canyon. One year prior, 43 year old Sasha had left her coveted but demanding studio job in Los Angeles and moved to a small island off Cape Cod to live a simpler quieter life. There she had fallen in love with a craftsman who specialized in restoring woodwork in historic homes. They moved in together and all seemed perfect until he very abruptly returned to his former wife. Sasha was devastated. She told her California friends that she felt that romance and magic were now gone forever. It was time to settle into arid middle age.

The concerned friends flew her out to the West Coast and threw her a breakup gala titled "Hot, Hot, Hot!", a theme which worked on several levels. One, her romance had gone bad in a frigid cold New England winter and the warm California climate was a much-needed tonic. Second, the friends wanted to remind Sasha that, despite feeling like an old rug, she was in fact still "hot". All elements of the party were designed to help her cast off the gloom of romantic defeat. Food was hot and spicy Mexican: chicken enchiladas, Mexican rice, beans and flan. Drinks were kicky salty margaritas.

And a sexy dance teacher was hired to teach the party guests how to dance the salsa. The bacchanalia culminated with a fire pit in which Sasha burned all of her photos of her departed woodsman. The party's centerpiece, a mounted deer head – her former boyfriend's first kill which she took from his home – also ended up in the fire pit in commemoration of her return to being single. "It was primitive and over the top," she said. "But it shook me out of the rut I was in and helped me to move on."

The Perfect Margarita
1 1/2 oz Tequila
3/4 oz Triple Sec
Splash of sour mix and/or fresh lime juice
Blend with crushed ice. Serve in glass dipped in kosher salt.

Black Bean Dip
1 can refried black beans
1 can whole black beans (rinsed and strained)
1/4 cup salsa (mild, medium or hot—you choose!)
8-10 drops hot pepper sauce
1/8 cup finely diced white or yellow onion
2-3 sprigs fresh cilantro, finely minced
1 clove garlic (finely minced or crushed)
1/2 cup shredded cheese (cheddar or monterey jack)

Combine all ingredients (except shredded cheese) in a microwave-safe dish. Microwave on high for approximately 3-5 minutes, or until heated through. Sprinkle shredded cheese on top, and microwave again for 30-45 seconds, or until cheese is melted. Serve with tortilla chips.

Chocolate Party
Chocolate works on many levels as the perfect theme for a divorce celebration. First and foremost, divorcing people are usually pleasure-deprived. They need the fix that chocolate offers. When we

eat chocolate, endorphins are released in our brains. Scientists even claim chocolate gives us more pleasure than sex, a comforting thought for those who may be living a celibate life.

Chocolate, like life, is also rich and mysterious. Cocoa beans must descend into rot and decay before they can be turned into chocolate. And then, how sweet it is! The divorcing one can find much symbolism in this process.

As a fun party activity, have your guests revel in all the Reasons Why Chocolate is Better Than Sex. Before the party, write as many reasons as you can think of, each on a small piece of paper. Put them in an empty chocolate box. Pass the box around. Have everyone take turns picking one out and reading it aloud. Encourage spontaneous ideas if guests want to add their own. Here are some to get you started:

Reasons Why Chocolate Is Better Than Sex
You can make chocolate last as long as you want it to.
You can have chocolate even in front of your mother.
Chocolate satisfies even when it has gone soft.
You can safely have chocolate while you are driving.
If you bite the nuts too hard the chocolate won't mind.
Two people of the same sex can have chocolate without being called nasty names.
The word "commitment" doesn't scare off chocolate.
You can have chocolate on top of your workbench/desk during working hours without upsetting your co-workers.
You can ask a stranger for chocolate without getting your face slapped.
With chocolate there's no need to fake it.
Chocolate doesn't make you pregnant.
You can have chocolate at any time of the month.
Good chocolate is easy to find.
You can have as many kinds of chocolate as you can handle.
You are never too young or too old for chocolate.
When you have chocolate it does not keep your neighbors awake.
With chocolate size doesn't matter.

As for food, consider serving mole, a Mexican dish of chicken cooked in a chocolate sauce. It sounds horrendous, but it's actually extremely tasty. For dessert, offer fabulous flourless chocolate cake or chocolate tart. Both are out of this world.

For an extra touch of chocolate, serve hard liquor like tequila or scotch in chocolate shot glasses (available from amazon.com). Party favors can be chocolate bars imprinted with "Happy Divorce" from chocolatefantasies.com.

Flourless Chocolate Cake
8 oz. semi-sweet chocolate, coarsely chopped
1/2 cup (1 stick) + 1 tsp unsalted butter
1/2 tsp vanilla extract
3/4 cup granulated sugar
4 eggs, separated
2 tbsp powdered sugar
1/2 cup whipped cream

Heat oven to 375 degrees. Line bottom of a 9-inch round cake pan with parchment paper and grease with 1 tsp. butter. In a small saucepan melt chocolate and remaining butter over low heat. Stir in vanilla, then remove from heat. In a bowl, mix 1/2 cup of the granulated sugar with the egg yolks. In another bowl beat egg whites until soft peaks form. Slowly add remaining granulated sugar to egg whites and beat till peaks are stiff. Using a plastic spatula, gently add the yolk mixture. Stir in melted chocolate. Pour batter into the pan. Bake 35 to 40 minutes until fork inserted in center comes out dry. Let cake cool, then upturn on a plate and dust with confectioners' sugar.

Boy Toy Party
A favorite with women, the Boy Toy party is all about looking at gorgeous men. If you want a total blast, hire male dancers. For a more dignified event, you could stage a fashion show featuring yummy male models. A stag party in reverse, this party works best

if cocktails and hors d'oeuvres are served first, followed by the show.

If the divorcing one is ready to date, you could also instruct each guest to invite along an unattached man for general consumption. It's a great way to recycle romantic partners. And the law of averages suggests that romance will be ignited at such an event.

A fun game for the erotic party is the Peter Pecker Doll and Game. This is a life-size blow up fellow with a 12" penis. Guests take turns doing a ring toss on to said member. Yeah, this is out there. With the right crowd, it could be a blast. It's available from www.bachelorette.com.

Or give your guests the following Sex Quiz. The winner gets a sexy prize.

PARTY SEX QUIZ

1. The most popular flavor of edible underwear is:
A. Chocolate
B. Cherry
C. Lemon
D. Strawberry
Answer: B

2. Ithyphallophobia is which of the following?
A. The study of insect erections
B. The fear of seeing an erect penis
C. The fear of having an erect penis
D. The fear of seeing, thinking about or having an erect penis?
Answer: D

3. Which famous woman, known for her parade of lovers, confessed to a friend that she had never had an orgasm?
A. Mae West
B. Marilyn Monroe

C. Madonna
D. Anais Nin
Answer: B

4. Formicophilia is best defined as:
A. An expert at filling out forms.
B. A lover of formica.
C. A fetish for having sex on formica floors.
D. A fetish for having small insects crawl on one's own genitals.
Answer: D

5. Besides humans, which species is the only other one who has sex for pleasure?
A. Monkeys
B. Whales
C. Dolphins
D. Honeybees
Answer: C

6. The first couple ever shown in bed together on prime time television was:
A. Lucy and Desi Arnaz
B. John Lennon and Yoko Ono
C. The Honeymooners – Jackie Gleason and Audrey Meadows
D. Fred and Wilma Flintstone
Answer: D

7. Which of the following female insects has no sexual opening and has a vagina drilled by the male's curved penis?
A. Scorpion
B. Louse
C. Bedbug
D. Spider
Answer: C

8. The word "fuck" derives historically from an English edict to:
A. Fornicate until the Christmas keg arrives
B. Fornicate under command of the king
C. Freedom under chosen kings
D. None of the above
Answer: B (The country was severely underpopulated at the time.)

9. A lot of sex can result in:
A. Reducing depression
B. Relieving headaches
C. Preventing plaque build-up
D. All of the above
Answer: D

10. The most popular American bra size is currently:
A. 34B
B. 34C
C. 36B
D. 36C
Answer: D

Condom Party

A condom Divorce Party is pretty outrageous but if the breakup was long and painful, it's a great way to blow off steam.

Ask the guests to bring sex-related gifts, from lotions and creams to sex toys and games. Or ask everyone to bring the most outrageous condom and have them compete for a prize. This will be a good way to kick start the party.

Also, decorate the party space with suggestions for "things to do with a condom". Put out paper and markers and invite guests to add their own ideas with a prize for the most original idea.

Examples of Things to Do With a Condom:

- Blow up the condom, knot it and use as a neck pillow on a long plane flight

THE DIVORCE PARTY HANDBOOK

- Fill with icing to ice a cake
- Inflate a bunch and twist into balloon animals to amuse small children
- Leave one under your office enemy's desk and make sure the boss sees it
- Fill with toothpaste and take on vacation – you don't have to schlep the entire tube
- Fill with crushed ice and use as a cold pack
- Emergency tourniquet
- Use to tie back your hair in a ponytail on a hot day
- Hang from both ears like hoop earrings and see if anyone notices• • this is a surefire ice breaker at a party
- Pool floaty for your pet mouse
- As a last meal serve your ex a plateful of fried calamari, toss in a condom or two and see if he notices
- Safe sex (duh)

As for other party activities, a penis *piñata* is always lots of fun. Instead of filling it with candy, fill it with a plethora of condoms of all sizes, colors and textures. Or have a water balloon fight using condoms of course. If it's nighttime, the neon ones blown up as balloons can be especially effective.

You can also turn the lights out and pass around a flashlight. Everyone has to tell an embarrassing sex secret. Or have each guest write a confession on a piece of paper and they are all put in a hat. They are drawn out and read one by one. The group has to try to match the confessions with the confessors. If things get hot, hand out Penis Popsicles. These are a Divorce Party favorite. You can make them yourself using molds available at funsextoys.com.

The sexy party cries out for a signature cocktail. (See p.21.)

For food, select sexy food. An easy and inexpensive solution is sexy pasta, which is pasta shaped as boobs or penises. Sexy pasta can be purchased from chocolatefantasies.com. Party favors and prizes for the sexy party are easy. Go for sexy items like:

Penis lollipop bouquet
Emergency condom key chain
Penis eyeglasses
Bride and penis chocolate gift set
Pecker lipstick
Penis cookies
Ball and chain
Gummy dicks
Chocolate oysters
Gummy love cuffs
Gummy whip
Penis party bubbles
Penis toothbrush
Mail stripper toothbrush
Male (or female) click and strip pen
Jelly Cucumber Vibe
Blow Me Party Blowers
"Kiss My Ass" chocolates - tiny chocolate lips kissing chocolate buttocks
All are available from chocolatefantasies.com.

Lingerie Party

A Lingerie Party can make a bold and timely statement. Traditionally the stuff of bridal showers, a lingerie party is a great way to dispel any post-divorce blues. This party mantra? It's time to move on! And moving on means throwing out that saggy old underwear and replacing it with new fabulous lingerie that can boost a woman's confidence and make her feel good about being alive. And who knows, she may be showing off her new undies to new suitors before too long.

 The whole tone of this party should be sensuous and feminine. Party decorations should be pink and white. The emphasis is on self-love, sex and pleasure.

 Include on the party invitation a request for all the guests to bring gifts of lingerie. Alternatively, ask everyone to chip in cash and give her a nice fat gift certificate to some lingerie emporium like Victoria's Secret. If you're throwing the party, you might take charge of buying the lingerie yourself. And even if she can't quite see herself in that sparkly red bustier, she can easily exchange the gifts for items more to her taste.

Party favors can be inexpensive sex toys or packages of neon condoms. Consider buying condoms which are embossed with personalized messages like " "Gather ye rosebuds while ye may", "Make Love Not War" or simply "Next!"

The food at this party is sexy and sensual both to look at and to eat. It could be food that is proven to boost sexual energy. Your menu might include aphrodisiacal shellfish like oysters or shrimp. A perfect cocktail to accompany all this splendor is the Cosmopolitan.

Deviled Oysters
Serves 6
1 pint oysters, with liquid
1/4 cup butter, melted
1 cup oyster crackers, crushed
1 medium green pepper, seeded and chopped
1/4 cup parsley, finely chopped
1 medium onion, grated
2 teaspoons Worcestershire sauce
2 hard-boiled eggs, chopped
3 eggs, lightly beaten
1/2 cup light cream
1 teaspoon Dijon mustard
1/8 teaspoon cayenne pepper
1/2 teaspoon salt

Combine all ingredients and toss well. Turn into a buttered 5 to 6 cup soufflé dish or casserole. Bake 30 minutes at 375 degrees until set and lightly browned. For individual servings, spoon mixture into buttered ramekins or scallop shells and bake for 15 minutes. To serve as hors d'oeuvres, bake in buttered oyster or clam shells for 10 minutes or until set.

Margarita Grilled Shrimp
(makes 4 skewers)
1 pound medium shrimp, de-veined and shelled
3 tablespoons of olive oil
2 large cloves of garlic, minced
2 tablespoons of tequila
1 tablespoon of lime juice
1/4 teaspoon salt
1/4 teaspoon crushed red chili pepper
3 tablespoons of cilantro, chopped

In a bowl whisk olive oil, garlic, tequila, lime juice, salt, red pepper, and cilantro. Add the shrimp to the marinade and coat well. Marinate for at least 30 minutes in refrigerator. Place shrimp on skewers. Grill shrimp on medium until pink. Do not over cook. Garnish with lime and cilantro.

Cosmopolitan
2 shots Vodka
1 shot Cointreau
1 shot cranberry juice
1 squirt of lime juice

Mix over ice and strain into cocktail glass.

Chapter Fourteen
"You've Got Friends" Party Themes

One of the most common laments of the recently divorced is that they feel isolated. They are left out of social gatherings if people are used to seeing them as half of a couple, or if they are uncomfortable with their unattached status. The Divorce Party is the perfect opportunity to nip all that in the bud, for everyone to show the newly single person that everyone accepts and supports what they are doing, and that any of the old stigmas surrounding divorce are swept aside. The party can also be thrown by the divorcing one to thank all the friends who have stood by them through the ordeal of separation. It's a way to say: thanks for letting me talk about it endlessly, and now I'm ready to move on.

Pamper Party
A Pamper Party is a perfect girlie get together. You can plan a day at a spa with a group of best friends. Or you could all wallow in the decadence of massages and nail treatments given in a home setting. Some large urban areas have mobile companies which provide this service but this party can be set up virtually anywhere. Simply approach nail salons and massage salons in your area and ask if they will host a home party.

To set the mood, consider offering sarongs and flip-flops as guests arrive so that everyone is in a relaxed pampered mood. Set up the party zone with a separate area for each masseuse or manicurist. Have sign up sheets so that guests can sign up for half hour sessions. In between the sessions make sure there's food and drink and conversation. Food should be light, healthy and delicious. For example, you could serve healthy little hors d'oeuvres like meats on skewers and vegetables with dips.

Pajama Party
Remember being thirteen and having those delicious sleepover parties which involved staying up all night giggling and gossiping. For some women, particularly those with old friends, a sleepover party can be the perfect tonic after a divorce, transporting the participants back to the glorious days of teenage bonding.

Have guests arrive already wearing their pj's, bathrobes and slippers. The evening is filled with Divorce Party games and girl talk.

Party favors might be old-fashioned hot water bottles which are perfect companions for those who sleep alone. A nice one in a chamois jacket is available at www.vermontcountrystore.com. The food part is easy. Simply stock up on lots of late night junk food like pizza, Cheetos, Hershey bars and popcorn.

Later in the evening create a huge group bed on the living room floor with lots of blankets and quilts and pillows strewn on air mattresses. Then snuggle down to watch rented video favorites like "Thelma and Louise" and "Waiting to Exhale". Avoid anything gooey or sentimental like "Love Story" or "An Affair to Remember". The point is to bond, not blubber.

A Roast
An old-fashioned roast is a wonderful way to boost a newly single friend's spirits, something that may be sorely needed at this time. Surround him or her with supportive family and friends who will shower them with appreciation and remind them of how much they are loved and admired as they move on as an unattached person.

Roasts typically start out with cocktails followed by food. Then everyone settles down for the fun part of the evening. Guests take turns to stand up and talk about what they love about him or her, perhaps sharing a special experience they had together. Some might want to prepare something in advance. Others may come up with spontaneous memories.

The food revolves around the "roast" theme. Roast chicken. Roast potatoes. Roasted vegetables.

Roast Chicken:

> Good roast chicken is very simple to make. Buying a good chicken is crucial. Kosher chickens are especially good. After rinsing the bird, pat it dry and salt it inside and out. Push sprays of fresh herbs under the skin and rub it all over with olive oil. Meanwhile heat the oven to 500 degrees and roast the chicken for around 30 minutes. Turn the heat down to 350 for another half hour or so. Don't overcook or undercook. It will be juicy, crispy, tender, and altogether yummy.
>
> Serve the chicken with potatoes roasted with the chicken in the juices at the bottom of the pan and roast vegetables which are simply tossed with oil and roasted for fifteen to twenty minutes in the 350 degree oven.

For dessert, roast s'mores or just plain marshmallows on an outdoor barbecue.

Shop 'Til You Drop Party

Divorcing people often yearn to reclaim their identity or even morph into a new identity. To help your pal with her personal makeover, arrange a shopping party. Take along a group of friends who will help her purchase a whole new wardrobe to match her new life. Have the shopping expedition culminate at a restaurant for a congratulatory dinner.

Post Marriage Garage Sale

Garage Sales can be lots of fun, especially if all the friends help out, aided by a big cooler of libations. Jettison all that ugly furniture that you never really liked, but that your spouse loved. If he or she left behind any clothes, sell them for a dime. If you want to really amp up the party atmosphere, advertise the event as a post divorce sale.

Lost Weekend
If your friend is stuck in post-divorce blues and spends his nights alone in his apartment watching movies or worse, staring at the cracks on the ceiling over his bed, consider jump-starting him out of his doldrums for a post-divorce weekend party. Las Vegas is a great choice for this kind of event. There are even companies that will organize all aspects of the party for you, including transportation, drivers, itineraries, entrance fees, etc.

Jeremy's Party is the perfect example. Months after his divorce was final, Jeremy was still depressed and refusing to date. He felt he'd never have a relationship again. His friends were getting worried. Jeremy had always been a neat freak. But now he was holed up in his home living on his computer and becoming more OCD than ever. His lawn was meticulously maintained, his bushes trimmed to perfection.

Jeremy's Divorce Party became a kind of intervention. It began with a stretch hummer whisking him off with his pals to Las Vegas. Along the way a butler served the men cocktails. Once there, Jeremy was taken for a luxury massage – it was the first time he'd been touched in months. Afterwards they all went to a comedy club where a comedian put on a special divorce themed show for Jeremy. Female guests showed up for a blow out party complete with Jeremy's favorite food and a custom cocktail, "Let It Rip!" The friends toasted Jeremy and reminded him how he was there for them at tough times in their lives. The night culminated with Jeremy facing his biggest fear – a rollercoaster. He was taken on the infamous elevated Vegas roller coaster where he had to "let go" for the first time in years.

Sail Away
Another good Divorce Party getaway is a cruise with a group of pals. For example, residents of Southern California can take a three day

cruise to Mexico at a surprisingly low cost. This is a fun take on a bachelorette party, a chance to laugh, drink, play and cry surrounded by friends and lots of food. Cruises provide a wide variety of activities and entertainment and can be excellent therapy for someone in the middle of a big life change.

Out with the Clutter Party

While once the domain of feng shui masters, the power of de-cluttering one's personal space has become more widely recognized in recent years. Clearing out the clutter can help create the sense of new beginnings, opening up space for new life and new experiences.

Just as the community would once rally to help raise a barn, your crowd can gather in the newly single person's home to help them de-clutter. Move from room to room getting rid of anything that hasn't been used in the past year. Empty out the bathroom cabinets with all those depressing old medicines. Shove any frumpy old clothes into bags and give them to the homeless. And if you find anything belonging to the ex, ceremoniously toss it in the garbage. After the purging is done, have a party!

Tea Party

This party would be perfect for the woman who likes order, is restrained in her emotions, and enjoys the company of her own sex. The group might congregate at a restaurant or hotel that serves a formal afternoon tea. Or the tea can be held at a private home.

Here's what you should serve. Tea, of course. Lots of it in different strengths and blends. Finger sandwiches. Small cakes. Scones with jam and clotted cream.

A Tea Party is more than just a nice way to sit around and have conversation. The truth is Tea has more caffeine than coffee and has long been a socially sanctioned stimulant for the British. The Tea Party can also reaffirm the value of coping with adversity with style and dignity.

Party favors could be Personalized Tea Bags. While generally sold as wedding favors, this cute little item can be easily adapted for a Divorce Party by adding your own cryptic message. Weddingfavorsunlimited.com offers one with a Bride and Groom on it. Simply put a black cross through the happy couple and change the words "Just Married" to "Just Divorced".

Perfect Cucumber Sandwiches
Combine dill and mayonnaise in a small bowl and spread on de-crusted bread squares. Pile on thinly sliced cucumber and sprinkle with kosher salt.

Garden Party

A garden luncheon party would be a wonderful way to celebrate a divorce especially if the invited guests camped it up and wore hats and dresses. Tables would be set up in a lovely garden setting where a simple elegant lunch would be served. Centerpieces could be arrangements of flower seed packets which would be given to the guests as favors. Guests might be asked to bring gifts that the unbride could use in her garden, whether it be plants, tools or birdhouses.

Another fun gift idea which might be purchased as a group is an intriguing item available from Scotland. Tiny plots of land on the Glencairn Estate are now available for purchase from www.buyagift.co.uk. For a small amount of money, the recipient gets not only a certificate verifying the land ownership but the legal right to use the title Laird or Lady. ("Laird" is the equivalent of the English title "Lord").

This is the perfect gift to present at the end of a dignified luncheon party. And what a great way for the newly single person to stand out from the dating crowd. Imagine introducing oneself as Lady Martha.

Girlfriends Rule

Debora, an engineer, decided to throw a Divorce Party as a thank you to the friends who had helped her through the process. Debora wore a tiara and a t-shirt that read "unencumbered". For each guest she made several personalized magnets including one that proclaimed "Girlfriends Rule" and placed them in a hand painted box stenciled with "Friends are the flowers of life."

She tied sayings written on card stock to the strings of helium balloons and placed them all around the house. These included: "In prosperity our friends know us. In adversity, we know our friends"; "If you obey all the rules, you miss all the fun" – Katherine Hepburn; "If it's a woman, it's caustic. If it's a man, it's authoritative" – Barbara Walters.

One of the guests made her a cake with a groom face down in the icing run over by a pickup truck.

A Celebration of Liberation and Libation
One day Tara's husband came home and told her he wanted a divorce because he was in love with another woman. He had been in contact with an old girlfriend from high school and wanted to rekindle the flame. This hit Tara like a runaway train. They had been married for ten years. She had put him through college, working two jobs and postponing having children.

Tara was shattered. She felt old, discarded and thoroughly unattractive. She went to stay with her sister Adrienne in Salt Lake City, Utah to recover. Adrienne took one look at Tara and decided it was time her wrecked sibling realized there were whole new possibilities available to her. A week later, Adrienne threw Tara a wild Divorce Party with the theme, "A Celebration of Liberation and Libation". Around fifty-five people showed up, dressed in everything from togas to formal gowns. All were unmarried, a prerequisite for attendance. At the door everyone had to do a shot of "Adios Mother" to gain entrance. Women were festooned with playboy bunny ears, men with gold Caesar crowns. There was an open bar, strobe lights, black lights, the whole party package.

Besides having the time of her life, Tara met several people who had gone through similar rough divorces. Lots of men flirted with her which boosted her self-esteem. Best of all, she realized she was not alone and that there was life after divorce.

The party was one of those memorable events that the people present talked about for a long time after. Since then, several people have asked Adrienne to throw similar parties for others going through post-divorce hell.

Black and Red Party
Just after her 40th. birthday, Teresa's husband left her and took up with a much younger woman. His explanation to Teresa was that she was past her childbearing years. Teresa was devastated. Hadn't they agreed for years that they both didn't want children? Teresa's workmate friend Diana felt something proactive needed to be done. Diana decided to throw Teresa a Divorce Party, hoping the bash would help her friend see something positive in her sudden singlehood.

Although both men and women were invited, all the men declined and the party quickly became fodder for conversation at the male-dominated local pub. The local baker couldn't stop laughing when Diana ordered her special divorce cake. On top were a bride and a decapitated groom. The head was hidden in the cake somewhere and whoever got it, won a prize!

The party was raucous and involved plenty of alcohol, much like a bachelorette party. The ex-bride was made to wear a t-shirt that said "Born to Flirt". The decorations were black and red. Black symbolized the death of a burned out flame. The red symbolized a new freedom.

Afterwards, Teresa took the cake decoration home and kept it displayed in a glass case. She enjoyed it immensely when her ex came over and asked what it was all about. As she put it, "These are the little moments that make life worthwhile."

Portrait Party
A beautiful portrait is a powerful tool which can help the divorced woman re-connect with herself. This party begins with the girlfriends helping the newly single woman get ready for a session with a portrait photographer taking pictures of her alone and her with

her friends. After she's dressed, hair and makeup done, the photographer arrives for her photo session. Afterwards there's a party. Alternatively the party can be picked up a week or so later when the photos are displayed and the final portraits are chosen.

A Night On the Town
Some people choose to celebrate their divorces with an evening out with friends. It's easy and inexpensive, especially if everyone picks up their own tab. David has an annual dinner on the date of his wedding every year. The commemorative dinner always takes place at Hooters. "It makes me smile," he says.

Vicky finally ended her marriage after finding a condom in her husband's wallet. When she confronted him, he said he was holding it for a friend. It was the last straw for Vicky. Her husband had been prone to violence. Although she knew that bringing her young son up by herself wasn't going to be easy, it was the better way to go. After the split she had a night out with her friends partying at a restaurant. "It was casual but something I'll never forget" she remembers. " I felt happy and relieved that the nightmare was over."

One fun idea for a friends' night out is to go to a Karaoke club with private rooms. A huge hit in Tokyo, these establishments are springing up all over the U.S. You simply pay by the hour to rent a private karaoke room where you and your friends can sing your heart out. This is a lot less embarrassing than doing it in front of strangers. Take the breakup song list and let it rip. (See p.43.)

A fun game specially designed for girls' night out events is "That Guy Game". It's a great way to meet men, have fun at their expense, or both. Participants draw cards and hit the town on a scavenger manhunt, searching for "mullet guy", "goatee guy", "tight pants guy", and all the rest. Available at thatguygame.com.

Chapter Fifteen
Unique Party Themes

Some breakups are so vivid that an unforgettable party is almost a necessity. The party is a way of breaking out of the tedium and anxiety of the struggle. In some cases divorcees even build their party theme around the core of the final feud. They say it can be very healing, kind of like lancing a boil. These parties tend to be idiosyncratic and knowing the back-story is essential to "getting it".

The Dating Game
Playing off the popular TV show, the evening begins with the divorced woman's friends on a pretend TV set, talking about the fact that she didn't do such a good job the first time around, but that there are plenty of other chances for her to do it right. Then the divorcee is told that there are three potential candidates for her to consider – not for a relationship, certainly not for marriage, just for a night out on the town. One by one, three men concealed behind a screen or curtain are questioned about love, life and women. The divorcee then decides which, if any, of the men are going to be invited on a bar crawl with the women later.

Fireworks Party
Fireworks parties are big business in the U.K. where the climate does not usually present the kinds of hazards which make fireworks displays tightly restricted in the U.S. A new trend is to throw a Divorce Party which culminates with a customized fireworks display. Steven Button, Managing Director of Leeds' The Great Northern Fireworks Company, says divorcees decide what they want to say to

the world and the company makes up the letters. "There are certain things we won't do with the letters. We have been asked to put the ex-partner's name and a nasty description of what they are like in lights but we refused. Usually we do "Free", "Free Again" or "Free at Last". Both women and men have requested this kind of public statement."

The Fireworks Divorce Party can be especially effective if there is still acrimony between the couple. Imagine the lonely ex sitting alone in his bare apartment eating a TV dinner when suddenly the night sky is ablaze with a firework display celebrating his absence. It certainly gets the message across loud and clear.

Roller Coaster Party

Ever notice how most people step off roller coasters with big grins on their faces? A rollercoaster ride is guaranteed to shake even the bleakest person out of the doldrums. And it's a great location for a Divorce Party outing. There is just no way anyone can remain in a state of ennui while riding the rails at a hair-raising speed.

Simply seek out the biggest and best roller coaster you can find within driving distance and then invite all of your friends to come along with you. You will experience the entire spectrum of human feeling in just a few thrilling minutes. All of this can make for an intense emotional workout that is cathartic and liberating. For some it's even a life-changing experience as primal fears are faced and conquered.

Afterwards, celebrate by going to a nearby cantina, reliving the terror of it all–the roller coaster that is, not the marriage!

Botox Party

Botox parties have gained popularity in the past few years. No matter where you live, you can probably access a qualified person willing to come to a private home to give Botox treatments. However, this should be thought through carefully when melded with a Divorce Party. The last thing anyone wants to convey to a divorcing person is that they need to change their appearance to be happy. On the other hand, a little rejuvenation, even on a superficial level, might help raise the spirits of one exiting a relationship.

Like the Pamper Party, guests will move between the treatment areas and the party areas where food and libations flow freely. For party favors, how about handing out one of modern life's miracles, a semi-permanent lipstick, to finish off the new look?

Hogs and Kisses
This is a fun theme for an easy low cost party. The theme centers on hogs and kisses – a great combination.

As guests arrive, offer them plastic pig snouts to strap on if they want to get into the full piggie mood (available from qualitybargainz.com). A fun party game is to have everyone confess who in the world they would most like to kiss and why? This can range from Leonardo diCaprio to their best friend's husband.

On the menu is ham (recipe for baked ham), barbecued pork sausages or pork chops, anything from the pig family. Dessert is chocolate tart topped by Hershey's kisses.

Music can be anything by the band Kiss. Party favors are boxes of chocolate kisses, fun pig gifts (healingbasket.com), or raunchy inflatable love pigs (meatcannon.com).

Chocolate tart
9-inch pie shell
1/2 cup milk
7 ounces bittersweet chocolate, chopped
2 small egg yolks
7 1/2 ounces crème fraîche

Preheat oven to 325 degrees. Lightly whip egg yolk with the crème fraîche. Set aside. Bring milk to boil, stirring continuously. Turn off heat. Add bittersweet chocolate to milk, stirring until chocolate is completely melted. Slowly add crème fraîche mixture to chocolate mixture, blending thoroughly. Pour into 9-inch shell. Bake in oven for 25 minutes. Remove tart from oven. After cooling to room temperature, place in refrigerator and chill for at least 2 hours before serving. Top with whipped cream and Hershey's chocolate kisses.

Inner Brat Party

For many of us, finding our inner child may better be described as finding our inner brat. And what better time to revert to childhood than the aftermath of an important breakup, a time when many people let rip, scream and stomp like two year olds.

Guests invited to the Inner Brat Party should be encouraged to wear t-shirts, shorts, jeans, and basic play clothes preferably in bright primary colors. Games center on letting the inner brat emerge in all his glory. The point is to play hard and get all the emotions out. Tantrums are welcome, as are bouts of crying.

Have cartoons playing on TV monitors in all the rooms. And rig up various play activities. For example, you could rent a trampoline to recreate that memorable scene in the movie "Big" where Tom Hanks wowed the uptight urban femme by jumping on a trampoline. Your guests could loll around in playpens sucking lollipops or in kiddie pools filled with water and water guns.

For more active play you could spray each other with shaving foam (best if done outdoors). Or fly kites if it's a windy day. Or set up a bubble machine to fill the air with bubbles. In some cities you can also rent adult size rocking horses and rock and vent as a group.

For entertainment, you could do something totally silly like hire a Sesame Street character to show up. Party favors are easy. Buy everyone a teddy bear to take home and cuddle.

A "D" Party

After a painful divorce, Toni threw a memorable Divorce Party at her home in Queensland, Australia. The party had a "D" theme. Everyone had to dress up as something starting with "D". One guest came as a doctor, another as a drunk, another as a disabled person in a wheelchair. Toni herself dressed up as the ultimate divorcee, Ivana Trump. Anyone who didn't wear a costume had to wear a dunce hat. Both men and woman were invited because Toni found that her male friends were just as helpful in getting her through her separation as the females.

In the center of the party space, Toni put a skeleton resting in a chair with a sign next to it: "Waiting for the Perfect Man". She also set up a dartboard with a blow up photo of her ex's head on it. Everyone threw darts and whoever was closest to the bullseye won a prize. By the end of the night, the picture was completely shredded. Toni gathered up the scraps of paper and mailed them to her ex. She also decorated her car with a "Just Divorced, Single and Loving It" and sprayed it with fake snow.

She had two *piñatas*. One was a penis. The other was a voodoo doll which she made herself. She stuck labels all over it with curses like "saggy jowls", "love handles", etc. For dessert, Toni had a divorce cake topped with a female figure standing on top of a male figure.

Toni said her Divorce Party was a night to remember, perhaps the best memory she has of her marriage. "It was long enough after the separation that I'd finally realized what a complete idiot my ex was," she said. "The party was a celebration of finally getting him out of my life."

She now always advises people recovering from a failed marriage or relationship to throw a breakup party. "I guess having your friends around you at a wonderful a party thrown just for you makes you remember that you are a good person and that you are liked even though the person you married can no longer see that."

Just Desserts

This party is easy on preparation and is perfect for a spur of the moment party. The theme congratulates the divorcing one on having given the ex his or her just desserts. The food is, of course, just desserts. Everyone gets to bring their own dessert favorite which is served with bucketfuls of bubbly champagne.

Eat Your Troubles Away

Eating can be a great way to soothe a bruised heart. Instead of turning into a couch potato eating gallons of ice cream, focus this desire into a party that is one big food extravaganza. Invite every guest to contribute something fabulous, something they love to make. Make sure there is a good balance of hors d'oeuvres, main dishes, salads and desserts. Encourage decadence because the whole point of this party is unabashed hedonism. If the group is small, you could invite everyone to come and cook together. You could also hire a chef who will cook for the party at the same time as he or she shares cooking tips with the guests.

For unique party favors, you could make up a commemorative recipe book for everyone which includes recipes for all the food in the feast. The book title might be: Eat, Drink and be Merry...and Eat Your Troubles Away, A Celebration of Susan's New Life.

"Where's the Beef?" Party
"Where's the Beef?" is a party theme for the divorcing person who found their partner lacking in substantive ways. It would be the perfect choice if the ex is a vegetarian.

Party food of course will be meats – delicious ribs, juicy lamb chops or gourmet burgers. Now is a time to emulate those supermodels chomping into juicy burgers on TV commercials. Revel in the pleasure of eating meat, marking a return to a full red-blooded life.

Entertainment for this party should be something beefcake, like a hunky male dancer, the kind who perform at bachelorette parties. For party favors, choose something fun and offbeat like those little wind-up walking denture toys or coupons for double cheeseburgers at a popular local hamburger joint.

Doggie Divorce Party
Divorce battles centering on pet custody are becoming more common. In fact dozens of law schools around the country - including Harvard, Georgetown, and Yale – now offer animal law classes that have segments on pet custody. And at least two law firms in California have partners who specialize in the area.

Sometimes the battles get ugly. Take the case of Gigi - a pointer-greyhound mix living in San Diego - who captured national attention when her former guardians went through a difficult divorce using the dog, say critics, as a pawn. A joint-custody agreement wasn't working and both wanted to be the primary caretaker. An animal behaviorist was brought in by the court to do a "bonding study". A "day in the life of Gigi" video was even presented by the wife's divorce lawyer which showed Gigi snoozing under the wife's chair at work and playing with her on the beach. After lengthy negotiations and more than $150,000 in legal fees, the court awarded full custody to the wife.

In pet custody cases like this, a great idea, and one which would bring some much-needed levity to the situation, would be to have a party with a theme pivoting on the central dispute, in this case a Doggie Party.

All guests would be invited to bring their pooches with them. On the menu would be hot dogs and hush puppies, with doggie pizza treats and dainty little dog confections for the canine crowd. Any leftovers would be packed in doggie bags for the guests to take home.

Plumbing Party

In too many cases, divorcing couples completely lose perspective as they battle each other to the bitter end. The struggle becomes deeply personal and each has to win no matter the cost. Divorce lawyers get rich off these grand extended battles. For example, one couple spent a fortune battling over who would get the hand painted Christmas ornaments they had picked up in Germany. The money spent on resolving this question could have financed trips to Europe many times over.

A typical struggle is over who will gain possession of the family home. In another nasty divorce reported in the San Diego area, the judge awarded the house to the husband. The wife was so irate that before turning over her keys, she had all the plumbing in the house ripped out. Sadly for her, it backfired. The husband pressed charges and she was forced to re-plumb the house at great expense. Whether the pleasure of gutting the house was worth the financial hit is not known.

A Divorce Party that followed this saga might have played with the plumbing motif. For example, party favors could be personalized toilet roll holders or personalized toilet paper with the husband's name inscribed on every sheet.

As for food, yes it's a stretch, but any dish that includes "plums" could work. This could any Chinese dish that has plum sauce, chicken plum salad, plum tart, BBQ with a plum glaze, etc.

Le Divorce

This party is built around a French theme. After all, the French are super cool about matters of the heart and can teach us a lot about handling divorce with style.

Decorations might be the poster for the movie "Le Divorce". Or make drawings of wedding cakes and hearts and wedding rings, then split the drawings in half and hang them all around the room.

Food has a French theme. Have French wine and cheese ready for arriving guests. Later have French fries, coq au vin, crepes, fondues, potages (soups). Dessert can be a fruit tartlette. Party favors could be French ticklers, French phrase books or that annoying book, "French Women Don't Get Fat."

Cookie Bake Off

This party is the ultimate cookie celebration and is a great way for female friends to congregate and regroup. There's something very primitive and comforting about women working together in the kitchen.

Ask each guest to bring their favorite homemade cookie recipe. Have supplies of all possible ingredients on hand so that party guests can break into small groups and make cookies, either individually or in groups. Everyone gets to sample the results and rates them on a scale of 1 to 10. There are prizes for the winners just like a county fair Bake Off.

A Red Party

The color red has long been celebrated as a symbol of power. It connotes confidence, boldness, assertiveness, all good traits for the newly single person. Red is the number one choice for sports car buyers. The Chinese believe the color red keeps evil away and is the preferred color for Chinese wedding dresses. Studies show that chickens exposed to the color red are happier and eat less food. Some chickens are even equipped with red contact lenses to raise profits.

The power of red makes it the perfect theme for a Divorce Party. A Red Party can symbolize a new chapter in the divorced person's life, the shedding of old skin and taking on a new vital identity. Everything about this party is red. Guests wear red clothes. They bring any gift they choose, as long as it's red. The food is all red in color. For example, you could serve bruschetta and roasted red peppers with cocktails followed by stuffed tomatoes or carrot soup or any red fish or meat.

If the party girl or guy needs "to see red" and vent anger, consider getting a red devil *piñata*, hand out a big stick, and let them go at it!

Bruschetta:
Bread
Olive oil
Basil
Whole fresh tomatoes
Onion
Fresh garlic
Chop/dice tomato (without seeds) and onion. Mince garlic. Place bread under broiler or in toaster until golden brown. Remove and put on a plate. Spoon tomato/onion/garlic over toast. Drizzle olive oil and sprinkle basil over the top.

Chapter Sixteen
Inspiring Party Themes

These parties are more serious in tone and are not for everyone. Yes there are some cliches here, but sometimes cliches are very comforting.

Silver Linings
The theme is of course "every cloud has a silver lining". The theme should be presented on a prominent banner. The party space can be festooned with silver garlands or strings of silver lights. Guests are asked to wear silver, whether it be clothes or jewelry. Tables are set with silver tableware and silver paper plates (available at most party stores.)

If outdoors, a nice activity for this party is to have the divorcing person write on small pieces of paper all the things she wants in her new life. These are pushed inside silver balloons which are then inflated and released into the sky.

As for gifts, all should be made of silver. These gifts will become part of his or her new household, daily reminders of the silver lining theme.

Believe In Magic Party
Many people coming out a failed relationship have a hard time believing they will ever again feel the magic that exists in life and love. That makes Believe In Magic a perfect Divorce Party theme. It will help remind any potentially jaded guests that magic is still all around us. You just have to be open to it.

Use a magic motif for your invitation. Ask your guests to wear black and white to set the mood for a magical evening.

As guests arrive, consider sprinkling them with magic dust. (Use gold or silver glitter dust which is available from any craft store.)

After the cocktails and food, one person can supervise the mixing of a spell titled "Get Over It". Simply purchase a Halloween plastic witch's cauldron. Partially fill it with dry ice. Then have party guests toss in mementos of the ex which can be photos, that disgusting hot sauce he left in the fridge, or even just blurted out memories.

The event culminates with a performance by a hired magician. Discuss with the magician beforehand how to tailor his act to match the party mood. For example, Los Angeles-based magician Andrew Goldenhersh does a very effective trick where he places a single egg on the ground, sweeps his cloak over it, and transforms it into a live chicken. It's always a crowd pleaser. Andrew's trick might be modified for a Divorce Party in the following way. Have him take something left behind by the departed one – like a pair of underpants or a favorite CD. With a sweep of his cloak, Andrew could miraculously transform the ex's possession into a Chippendales–style male dancer who ends up getting all the guests on their feet and dancing up a storm.

Scrapbook Party

At this party guests build a scrapbook tribute to the divorced friend. This is not just a nice party activity but will also result in a valuable keepsake which can be very comforting in the months to come. Have all guests bring photos or emails which show a unique side of him or her.

To prepare for this party, purchase a big scrapbook or photo album with clear sleeve pages and lots of tools like gel pens, stickers, glitter and glue. Lay them out on a big table. Throughout the party guests each build a page or more with mementos and inscriptions. Make sure everyone signs the first page.

Ideas for scrapbook elements:
Photos
Her favorite movie or song
Secrets
First kiss
Crushes
Letters
Special emails
Favorite food wrappers

Butterfly Party

There's a reason why butterflies have become popular adjuncts to weddings. The amazing metamorphosis of the caterpillar into a beautiful elegant butterfly is a great metaphor for the potential of we humans to transform our lives. That's what makes it the perfect motif for a Divorce Party celebrating change and new beginnings.

The butterfly party theme can be played out in a several unique ways. If your party girl is in agreement, the wedding dress can be transformed by a seamstress into a sexy cocktail dress which is presented to her at the beginning of the party. The newly single femme changes into it and makes a grand entrance. She might even rip up a photograph of herself wearing the wedding dress in its original form. Everyone applauds her metamorphosis and re-emergence into life as an attractive available woman.

Real butterflies can be released at some point. A nice touch is to give everyone a small box containing live butterflies and have them all released at once. Butterflies can be purchased online, for example at www.insectlore.com.

This company also supplies a kit to grow butterflies. The butterfly kits can be lovely party favors. Hand them out with packets of flower seeds which will grow into attractive gardens for the new butterflies. (For those who prefer party favors that are not alive, there is a wonderful variety of butterfly favors available at www.orientaltradingcompany.com.)

Alternatively, if the divorcing person is a gardener, consider setting up the butterfly garden as a group party activity. Simply select an area that is sheltered from wind and that receives plenty of sunlight. Then plant flowers which produce fragrant blossoms that will attract the butterflies with their nectar. Place a flat stone near the flowers for the butterflies to perch on and bask in the sun. And include a small container of muddy water where the butterflies can drink and socialize. If possible, also provide host plants like cabbages where butterflies can lay their eggs and caterpillars can be free to nibble on leaves. Once the garden is complete, have all the guests release butterflies into the garden.

You can also make up some posters with amazing butterfly facts and hang them around the party space. For example:

- A butterfly can TASTE with its feet.
- There are 120,000 different kinds of butterfly worldwide.
- As a butterfly metamorphoses from egg to caterpillar to pupa to butterfly, it increases its weight by a factor of 2700. (If a 7lb. human baby grew at this rate, it would end up the size of a double-decker bus).
- Monarch butterflies fly up to 2000 miles to winter in warmer climates. Many return to same tree where they were hatched.
- A butterfly has a long tongue called a proboscis which they uncoil and dip into the nectar at the center of each flower.

Flowers attractive to butterflies:
Pansy, violet, chrysanthemum, aster, milkweed, bougainvillea, dahlia, geranium, hibiscus, marigold, snapdragon, yellow sage and zinnia.

Love Party

A Love Party is a great way to let your newly divorced friend know that he or she still has volumes of love in his or her life, even though their significant other is history. A Love Party is easy to decorate. You simply have pink hearts and red roses everywhere. Ask guests to wear pink, red or white to match the décor.

It would be fun to make a buffet of pink food. That is not as hard as it might seem. Walk around any supermarket and you can see food that is pink like salmon, strawberries, grapefruit, shrimp, watermelon, red leaf lettuce, raspberries. You could decorate with pink and white daisies and offer Perrier fluo rose which is pink sparkling water. If you do serve anything with pastry, put a little beetroot juice in the mix and it will turn pink.

You could even rent a cotton candy machine so that fluffy pink cotton candy can be consumed.

For the perfect Love Party activity, get the popular children's book "Guess How Much I Love You" which is now available with an elegant adult cover. As a companion piece, buy a scrapbook and title it "Guess How Much We Love You". Have everyone at the party write in how much the divorcing person is loved accompanied by lists of all the reasons. This is a wonderful keepsake which will be cherished for many years.

A New Day Party

Party guests get this theme as soon as they walk into the party and see a banner proclaiming: The Rest of Your Life Is Just Beginning. The spirit is optimism and a sense of possibilities. A highpoint of the evening is the arrival of a Fortune Teller who tells everyone's fortune.

Party favors might be personalized fortune cookies. These are available from www.WeddingThings.com (if you can stomach it). Here are some ideas for your personalized fortunes:

- When one door closes, another one opens
- Lovers come and go, but true friends last forever
- In the dance of life, choose your partner wisely
- The love we share with friends is worth a fortune
- May good fortune bless all our lives
- A heart that loves is always young
- Fortune Cookie: $1; Being at (Michelle's) Divorce Party: Priceless

Dawn Beach Party

This party is only for the hale and hearty, so choose your guests carefully. The party plan is to meet at sunrise on a beach to watch the sun come up together and celebrate the dawn of the divorced person's new life.

This is a great time to cast into the ocean any mementos of the relationship like a ring or a letter or photograph. This can be done with some ceremony as a way of cleansing and purging.

If your guests are robust and up for it, line them up on the sand and have them run into the ocean like the Polar Bear Club, those Coney Island residents who since 1903 have plunged into the ice cold ocean every Sunday from October through April.

After the dip, make sure there is someone on hand with a camping stove fired up, ready to feed the swimmers eggs, hash browns and hot chocolate.

A Hiking Party

Some people far prefer going on a rigorous hike with friends than sitting around drinking and eating. Strenuous physical exercise produces endorphins, making a tough hike very pleasurable.

For example, in Southern California, a popular group hike is the trek up Mt. Baldy, the state's highest mountain. The hike is like walking up an endless flight of stairs, and involves some precipitous walking along "the devil's backbone", a narrow trail with steep slopes deeply plunging on both sides. But it's worth it. The peak is stunning. There are lots of boulder-strewn flat areas where the party can have a picnic and toast the newly single one for having climbed the mountain and for having traversed his or her way out of a difficult relationship.

For the picnic, pack plenty of protein like chicken legs, hummus with pita bread, cheeses, pasta salads and fresh fruit. Toast with something non-alcoholic like cranberry cocktail juice.

Chapter Seventeen
After the Party

The guests have gone home. And hopefully the party has brought closure to the party girl or guy. Divorce Parties can be a great reminder of the strength and value of "buddy systems". But the support doesn't stop now. There are a number of ways friends and relatives can continue to help the divorcing person through this transition, both in the short term and the long term.

The Morning After
Make sure friends chip in to help with the breakdown and cleanup in the aftermath of the event. If the party took place at the newly single person's home, this is crucial. He or she does not want to spend the first day of a new life tossing out bottles and cleaning up sticky spills.

Thank You Notes
If gifts were involved...don't forget to send thank you notes. Do it as soon as possible so it's out of the way. And if anyone used a digital camera to take photos, have them posted online and include the web address for print purchases with your thank you note. This is a nice way to keep the spirit of the event going, and for everyone to have tangible reminders of the strong friendships and relationships at the heart of it all.

As a last flourish on the morning after a party, consider putting an ad in the local paper announcing the divorce and stating that he or she is now officially and happily unmarried.

Help New Divorcee Notify the World

After the party friends might even help out with some of the boring parts of making the transition to singlehood. For example, she might want to send out notices to everyone about her new status, new name and new contact details. She might even send out divorce announcements. Readymade divorce cards can be found at greetingcarduniverse.com. Or have a card printed up. If the divorce is amicable, this is a great way to let friends know that everyone's fine and everyone's moving on. For example, "Mary and Peter Cuthbert announce their amicable divorce."

In addition, he or she might appreciate help with the boring but necessary task of making sure that all areas of their lives receive official notification of their change in marital status as well as any change in name, address and phone number. A copy of the divorce certificate should also be included where necessary.

Chapter Eighteen
Divorce Party Etiquette

Is it okay to throw your own Divorce Party?
Absolutely. In fact it might be just what the doctor ordered, a way to mark the end of a difficult and emotional time and the beginning of the rest of your life. But be sure and ask good friends to chip in and help just as you probably did when you got hitched.

Should the ex ever be invited?
Only under very rare circumstances would an ex be welcome. For example, celebrity divorce lawyer Dominic Barbara told the New York Times that one of his clients, whose name he wouldn't reveal, was throwing a Valentine's Day party to celebrate her divorce. The party was held at a four-star New York restaurant and was co-hosted by her ex-husband. Both parties are wealthy investment bankers who had divorced amicably. Their gesture indicated to their friends that their relationship was still cordial and there would be no problem inviting both of them to social events in the future.

Ex-Seagram's President Charles Bronfman and his wife had a similar event. The wealthy elderly couple invited all their friends to a cocktail party in a the Ritz Hotel in New York as a way of letting everyone know that the split was amicable and no one should feel the need to choose one friendship over the other, as often happens after a divorce.

I'm having a Divorce Party and would like to invite everyone who was a guest at our wedding. Is this a good idea?
There's a certain symmetry to the notion but... it's a bad idea. Keep your guest list to close friends and relatives who will get it. Not

everyone is comfortable attending this kind of event, especially the old aunties, with a few exceptions.

Is it okay to have my kids attend my Divorce Party?
Make it an adults only event. It might be confusing and even disturbing for young minds to take in a Divorce Party.

I'd like to have my Divorce Party the day after my divorce is final. My sister thinks it's too soon and that I should have a cooling off period first.
There are no hard and fast rules on scheduling. You should have your party when you feel you want and need it. Some people even do it during the divorce proceedings – it can be a refreshing interlude, especially if it's tough going. Others wait till all the dust is settled. Go with your instincts, and tell sis thanks but you can make your own decisions.

If a Divorce Party is to take place at a restaurant, who should pay? The host? Or should each person pay for themselves?
It's your choice how you want to handle it. If you're hosting, you pay. If you're simply arranging for everyone to get together, each person pays individually. You can spell it out in the way you word the invitation. "I am throwing..." is very different to "Why don't we all get together and..."

Is it okay to burn the ex's belongings at the party?
Burning things is very primitive and for many very satisfying. It's a form of simple therapy, carefully tossing things into the flames and watching them be consumed and obliterated. This can also be very empowering. We've heard of wedding dresses being burned at divorce parties, even the marital bed. One caveat...exercise caution and safety and don't let anyone get carried away with the process, no matter how exhilarating. Always burn in a safe and legal zone.

Is the Divorce Party a good time to share juicy gossip about the ex?
Be careful with this. Beneath the surface of most divorces there is a great deal of hurt and pain. You don't want to trigger any regressive

emotions that can bring the party girl or guy down. Even when we are done with a relationship, hearing that the ex is schtupping someone new can cause twinges of jealousy, anger or regret. Use your judgment and if you have any doubts, hold the gossip for another time when you can be sure its impact can be contained.

You just met a fabulous new person and are now a guest at a Divorce Party. Is this a good time to talk about your new love interest?
No. The last thing a newly single person needs to hear is how a pal is reveling in the bliss of love or passion. Keep the focus on them and their journey onward to find new loves.

This is my second divorce. Okay, I'm not good at the marriage thing. I threw a Divorce Party the first time around. Is it okay to have one this time?
Of course! You had a wedding the second time, didn't you? And better still, you're an old pro and will probably be able to whip up a great event since you know what worked at your first Divorce Party.

I found out I was pregnant after my ex and I split up. Is a Divorce Party a bad idea since I'll be six months pregnant?
Actually all the noise and good cheer should be good for the developing fetus. And both you and the baby will benefit from the support of the community around you.

I'm throwing a Divorce Party for my brother's ex-wife who's still recovering from his infidelity. My brother's annoyed and thinks I'm taking her side. Should I cancel the party?
I think you can take a clear position with your brother that you wish to support her as someone who has suffered in the breakup. He probably has his own reasons why he strayed from the marriage but I imagine you have made it clear to him that you do sympathize with her and that you want to continue to stand by her. Either he gets it, or he doesn't. Weigh this carefully however. It could have lasting repercussions.

My husband had an affair with a friend of mine Jennifer who was my Maid of Honor when we got married. He then dumped her for his hair stylist. Now Jennifer wants to come to my Divorce Party. What do you think?
Don't invite her under any circumstances. Why are you even talking to her?

I'm planning a surprise Divorce Party for my brother? Is this a good idea?
It depends on your brother's temperament and his current state of mind. It could be just what he needs. Or it could backfire and be a real downer. Talk it over with a guy friend of his and get a read on the situation. Surprise parties aren't always welcome.

Who should and shouldn't host a Divorce Party?
Divorce Parties can be hosted by anyone – the newly divorced person, their friends, their family, whoever. The only circumstance that seems distasteful might be if a toxic spouse whose behavior destroyed a marriage threw a divorce celebration. That might be hard to stomach.

I'm planning a Divorce Party and have invited my sister who is marrying a month later. She thinks I shouldn't have the party so close to her wedding.
That's your decision, not hers. One door closes and another one opens. Let her know nicely that your event will by no means cast a shadow over hers and that you will attend her wedding with the appropriate spirit and optimism. Tell her you won't be offended if she is not in the mood to attend your party and leave it at that.

My husband is using my Divorce Party plans as an indication of my bad character in our divorce proceedings. Do you think I should postpone the party till after the court date?
I would ignore it and carry on with your plans. Most judges will not care a hoot. Some might even empathize. Obviously you and your husband are not on the same wavelength – which is exactly why you're having a Divorce Party, n'est ce pas?

I'd like to ask my four onetime bridesmaids to host a Divorce Party for me. Sort of like life coming full circle. What do you think?
Bad idea. No one should be asked to host a party. Throw it yourself if no one offers.

My pals are organizing a Divorce Party and they asked me about shower gifts. I'm inclined to skip the gifts and have everyone chip in to buy twenty tons of fresh manure to be dumped in my ex's driveway. Is this okay?
Revenge is sweet. But I'd say skip the momentary thrill of the manure dump and use this occasion for more positive impulses…like going for the gifts. Select things your ex would never have appreciated and enjoy them.

I'm dying to have a Divorce Party but I don't want to spend a lot of money. How can I do it?
Concentrate on the fun aspects that cost nothing like the games, the music and a good bunch of pals who'll have a great time together. You can eat and drink cheaply. For example, go to a discount food warehouse and buy a case of wine and a stack of frozen pizzas. Or ask each guest to kick in $25 and splurge on champagne and trays of sushi.

I'm having a Divorce Party and my friends told me they are planning on having a dartboard set up with my ex's face as the bullseye. As each guest throws a dart, she or he can say what they dislike about him. This makes me uncomfortable.
Don't do anything that doesn't feel right. Tell your friends you don't want to trash your ex at the party. Also you may prefer not to rehash the breakup or answer questions. It's your party and you get to choose.

My gang always consumes a lot of alcohol at any social gathering. How do I set limits so as not to send dangerous drivers out on the road?
Make sure there are designated drivers. Or make it a sleepover party – get lots of blankets and pillows and sleeping bags. It could be fun. And have lots of strong coffee ready for them when they wake up.

Chapter Nineteen
Looking Forward

In the weeks and months following a Divorce Party friends and relatives should remember to help their divorced pal stay on a good track. There may be ups and downs ahead and they may continue to need support. Call them frequently. And be sure to invite them to social events. In the first months, close friends might even arrange to take turns preparing a meal and bringing it over to eat with their newly unattached pal.

Divorce is a time when a life has been changed irretrievably. But after the pain comes a new life. Divorce can be an opportunity for growth, a springboard to a new and better life. The party or ceremony is just the beginning.

Appendix

Divorce Party Supplies
www.divorcepartysupply.com
www.divorceshowerstore.com
www.cheriescloset.com
www.party-over-here.com
www.chocolatefantasies.com
www.amazon.com
www.bachelorette.com
www.party411.com
www.wholesalefavors.com
www.customwedding.com
www.orientaltradingcompany.com
www.healingbaskets.com
www.cafepress.com

Invitations
www.cjpaper.com
www.sandscripts.com
www.papermania.com
www.discount-invitations.com
www.evite.com
www.justsayitwithcards.com

411 at a Glance

CONTACT:_____PHONE:_____ E-MAIL:_____

Divorcee:

Party Host:

Party Site:

Caterer:

Cake Maker:

Music/DJ:

Entertainment:

Parking:

Party Supplies:

Flowers:

Photographer:

Videographer:

Portable Toilets:

Made in the USA
Columbia, SC
20 December 2018